THE

COURAGE
GAP

THE
COURAGE
GAP

· · · · · · · · ·

5
Steps to
Braver Action

MARGIE WARRELL, PhD

Berrett–Koehler Publishers, Inc

Berrett-Koehler Publishers, Inc.
1333 Broadway, Suite P100
Oakland, CA 94612-1921
Tel: (510) 817-2277
Fax: (510) 817-2278
bkconnection.com

ORDERING INFORMATION
Quantity sales. Special discounts are available on quantity purchases by corporations, associations, and others. For details, please go to bkconnection.com to see our bulk discounts or contact bookorders@bkpub.com for more information.
Individual sales. Berrett-Koehler publications are available through most bookstores. They can also be ordered directly from Berrett-Koehler: Tel: (800) 929-2929; Fax: (802) 864-7626; bkconnection.com.
Orders for college textbook / course adoption use. Please contact Berrett-Koehler: Tel: (800) 929-2929; Fax: (802) 864-7626.

Distributed to the US trade and internationally by Penguin Random House Publisher Services.

Berrett-Koehler and the BK logo are registered trademarks of Berrett-Koehler Publishers, Inc.

Printed in the United States of America

Berrett-Koehler books are printed on long-lasting acid-free paper. When it is available, we choose paper that has been manufactured by environmentally responsible processes. These may include using trees grown in sustainable forests, incorporating recycled paper, minimizing chlorine in bleaching, or recycling the energy produced at the paper mill.

Library of Congress Cataloging-in-Publication Data
Names: Warrell, Margie, author.
Title: The courage gap : 5 steps to braver action / Margie Warrell, PhD.
Description: First edition. | Oakland, CA : Berrett-Koehler Publishers, Inc., [2025] | Includes bibliographical references and index.
Identifiers: LCCN 2024028786 (print) | LCCN 2024028787 (ebook) | ISBN 9781523007240 (paperback) | ISBN 9781523007257 (pdf) | ISBN 9781523007264 (epub)
Subjects: LCSH: Self-actualization (Psychology) | Courage. | Self-confidence.
Classification: LCC BF637.S4 W368 2025 (print) | LCC BF637.S4 (ebook) | DDC 158/.1—dc23/eng/20240804
LC record available at https://lccn.loc.gov/2024028786
LC ebook record available at https://lccn.loc.gov/2024028787

First Edition
32 31 30 29 28 27 26 25 24   10 9 8 7 6 5 4 3 2 1

Book production: Susan Geraghty
Cover design: Ashley Ingram
Interior design: THE COSMIC LION

This book is dedicated to the courageous women
and men across the world who risk everything
to stand for freedom, ensuring others are
treated with dignity, can speak freely,
and fulfill their potential.

Let us honor their courage
by answering its daily call
in our own lives.

Contents

CONTENTS

STEP 3

Breathe in Courage

STEP 4

Step into Discomfort

STEP 5

Find the Treasure
When You Trip

CLOSING

Make Others Braver

Foreword

In my four decades–plus career in the military and now consulting with leaders across various sectors, I've witnessed many acts of extraordinary courage, from soldiers laying their lives on the line to protect others to leaders risking their livelihood to do what they believed was right. These experiences have solidified my belief in the innate capacity for courage within every individual. Yet for many this capacity remains largely untapped, evidenced by the dearth of courage in today's world.

We all experience moments when we know what we should do yet fail to do it. Even the most valiant among us sometimes struggle to be courageous. Fear of potential fallout clouds our judgment, fueling indecision, timidity, and sometimes outright cowardice. That's why the message of this book is so needed for this time, and Margie is the perfect person to deliver it.

Although Margie and I have traversed different paths, we've converged on the same belief: that in our efforts to protect ourselves, we can inadvertently become more vulnerable to greater dangers. Drawing on her unique mix of experience and expertise, Margie has crafted a five-step framework to operationalize courage that is both sophisticated and straightforward. Cutting through the hype, she has distilled the research into a realistic road map to closing the think-do gap between thought and action, between dreaming and doing.

What stops us from attempting to better our circumstances is not a lack of intellect or knowledge. Rather it is a lack of commitment to the values—and corresponding behaviors—to which we aspire to hold ourselves accountable. In an era when virtues such as character, integrity, and honor seem increasingly dispensable, this book serves as a rallying cry, urging us to take full ownership of our lives and realign ourselves to higher principles that embolden us to advance where many retreat or shelter in the status quo. Soldiers exemplify this principle when their commitment to protect freedom, defend their comrades, and retain respect for themselves keeps them from fleeing in combat—and so they brave danger.

We're all tasked with striving to embody the best version of ourselves. Although none of us are brave all the time, this book will equip you with the principles to be braver more often, utilizing your full agency and creating a life that honors your talents. Through relatable anecdotes and compelling insights, Margie will elevate your perspective to see *every* experience, particularly the most challenging, as a catalyst for growth and the greater good.

In a time fraught with division and disruption, *The Courage Gap* isn't just a book—it's a lifeline.

A note of warning: stepping into your courage gap won't be comfortable, but it is the worthiest of all endeavors. This book will help you take that critical first step . . . and then another, until you embody the courage you've admired in others, inspiring countless others to summon their own.

General Stanley McChrystal (US Army, Retired)

Preface

I've stood at the edge of my courage gap many times since I was a grubby-faced kid in the Aussie bush. And many times, I've balked. Yet I've also managed a few brave moments when I've fumbled nervously forward. Like the day I hugged my five younger siblings and parents goodbye, leaving life on my parents' dairy farm for university in "the city," the first in my family to do so. I was an insecure eighteen-year-old whose vision for my life extended little beyond our back paddock, but I was determined to expand it. That uneasy step emboldened future ones, from backpacking around the world after graduating to having four kids in close succession across multiple global moves.

Not all the experiences that have called for courage have been by choice. Like everyone, I've had my share of heartache and hardship that has shattered my mental maps of how life is "supposed to be" and left me awash in fear. Yet the situations that have tested me most, particularly those I'd naively assumed would never happen to me, have ultimately led to my greatest growth. The experiences in the last five years, testing and teaching me in new ways, have led me to write this book.

They began in the first days of 2020 as charred leaves rained down while I was hastily helping my parents pack their few precious belongings to evacuate wild bushfires in Australia. I recall thinking how hard it would be to top this as the "big news" story of 2020. Huh. By March 2020, my husband, Andrew, was hospitalized as one of Singapore's first COVID patients, and I was quarantined in our apartment there with our son Ben as our other three children, ten thousand miles away studying in the US, were suddenly homeless.

I've grieved my mother's long goodbye to dementia, made all the more wrenching by international travel restrictions that prevented my returning to Australia to see her for two long years. I also moved from Asia back to the US, after a decade away, and found it more difficult than I'd anticipated to reestablish life and community. The fact that I landed in the midst of a pandemic, pre-vaccines, didn't help. In parallel with that was adjusting to "free bird" status (my term for *empty nester*) as our four children spread their broad wings. Taking on a senior partner role in the board and executive advisory practice of a preeminent leadership consulting firm was another wholly new and broadening experience.

Not every challenge has brought me to my knees. Yet all have strengthened my belief that what most limits our lives and threatens our future is not external, but we ourselves: it is our undeveloped courage to take action despite our fear. Working with highly intelligent leaders has only further affirmed how our unaddressed insecurities, unfaced fear, and untamed ego ultimately leaves us—and those around us—less secure.

The backdrop of my roller coaster is a world that's weathered immense disruption and grown increasingly fragile, fractured, and fearful, leaving millions disconnected from their agency and socially isolated.

Writing this book has required stepping firmly into my own courage gap. On a few occasions, fear of falling short and being exposed as inadequate in helping you bridge the gap that caused you to pick up this book has engulfed me in a wave of vulnerability. Some might assume I'd be past that by now. After all, this is not my first author-rodeo. Not so. It's been in these moments that my mother's gentle wisdom—"Write to help, not to impress"—has brought me back to the call on my heart that inspired me to start out. I hope you'll sense that wisdom in the pages ahead. More so, I hope it will help you heed the siren call on your own heart, however loudly your fear urges you to dismiss it or shelter in place.

Thank you for opening yourself to the invitation of this book to step into the gap between who you are now and who you *can* be, between the life you're living and the highest and holiest vision of the life you aspire to lead. As you turn each page, imagine we're catching up over coffee or a pot of my favorite Earl Grey tea, or whatever takes your fancy. Because that's how I'll be writing it, knowing that you want to do more and be more, but that you sometimes pull warily back in the very moment you need to step bravely forward.

Mahatma Gandhi said, "The difference between what we do and what we are capable of doing would suffice to solve most of the world's problems."[1] Right now, the world needs your courage, not your perfection. It's my hope that the pages to come will help you find more of it.

Margie

PS. I thought you'd like to know that I pronounce my name with a hard G, as in Margarita. I've been trying to convince people that the drink (a favorite of mine) is named after me. No one's been buying it, but I'll keep trying.

THE
COURAGE
GAP

INTRODUCTION

Fear Creates the Gap. Courage Closes It.

Ever thought to yourself *If I just had the guts*? Or held back from speaking up, afraid of what might happen if you did? Or put off making a change, only to regret waiting so long?

Of course, I'm sure you've also had moments when you've put yourself "out there" despite your misgivings. But how often have you known what you *should* do, yet not done it? Or not soon enough.

Such is the human condition. We arrive in the world programmed more for self-preservation than self-actualization, more for fitting in than breaking out, more for seeking certainty than braving the far limb.

Yet we wouldn't have crossed vast oceans by the stars, traversed mountains in wagons, or set foot on the moon if we didn't have a capacity to act in the presence of fear and legitimate danger. So rest assured—no matter how daunting your challenges, how insecure you feel or cautious your personality, you've got all the raw materials for being braver more often than you have been until now. This isn't conjecture. Modern science verifies what the wise have long known: that courage—defined as consciously choosing to act in the presence of fear and potential risk, real or perceived—is a learnable skill and that like all skills, it can be developed with practice.[1]

Yet herein lies the challenge: we're living in a world where sensationalized news cycles are magnifying our perception of danger, preying on our fear, bombarding us with reasons to play it safe. Little wonder more people today depend on anti-anxiety medication[2] than ever before despite this being the safest time in human history to be alive.

We cannot intellectualize our way to courage. If we could, the world would be in better shape, examples of intelligent people making "unsmart" and ego-driven decisions would be less common, and courageous leaders willing to lay their power on the line for the principles they espouse would be less exceptional. After all, we have access to more knowledge on our phones than existed in all the libraries of the world when I was learning to read (and I'm not *that* old).

As intelligent as we are, we humans are governed more by emotion than by logic. And of all the emotions woven into our psychological DNA, fear is the most primal and potent. Of course, this is not breaking news. However, given the news that *is* breaking relentlessly around us, fear has seeped into every corner of our lives in ways it could not do even ten years ago when it wasn't so easy to hide behind a screen or huddle in echo chambers of self-protection. Along the way, fear has impaired our ability to discern degrees of risk, shuttered critical thinking, stymied civil debate, fractured social connection, and fueled a wholly noninclusive "cancel culture."

The pervasive cautiousness of our risk-phobic society[3] has only compounded this challenge: in our efforts to shield ourselves from risks, we've become more vulnerable to greater perils. Yet just as we are our greatest source of risk—in how we perceive and respond to the risks inherent in all aspects of life—we are also our greatest source of overcoming it. We do that every time we choose to close the gap between what we are doing and what we can do.

You might call it the *know–do gap*. Or the *think–do gap*. Or the *say–do gap*. Or the *who-you're-being-versus-who-you-can-be gap*.

I call it *the courage gap*.

Closing this gap is no small task. Rising above human instinct has always been a formidable endeavor. Even those who seem endowed with an extra "courage gene" are not invulnerable to fear, albeit in less conspicuous ways. You'll meet a few of these people in this book. Among them is retired Navy SEAL Alex Pease. I'll be weaving his inspiring yet wrenching story through the pages ahead, beginning with his arrival in the Venezuelan town of Guri.

* * * * * * * * * *

A six-hour drive from Caracas, the small town of Guri is unremarkable except for one thing—it's home to one of the world's largest dams, discharging nearly double the amount of water every second than discharged by Niagara Falls at high water. At the dam's base, water is forced into a gorge about one hundred yards wide and more than seven hundred feet deep, forming a violent Class 5 rapids navigable only by the world's most skilled whitewater kayakers.

In 1995, a team of five Navy SEALs embarked on a mission to test a relatively unproven capability at that time of navigating extreme rapids in small inflatable boats. Their expedition was based on the theory that rivers are the highways of rugged jungle terrain that's inaccessible by road. If SEALs could be parachuted into such environments with rafts, they could carry out missions that would otherwise be impossible.

Fear creates the gap between who you are and who you can be. Courage closes it.

Four of the five men were highly experienced operators with over forty years of experience between them. The fifth SEAL, Alex, was on his first mission fresh out of training. Although Alex was new to the SEALs, his years as a river guide had given him significantly more experience navigating extreme whitewater conditions and a stronger comprehension of the dangers in a river of that magnitude and the consequences of making any mistake. However, Alex was also acutely aware of his rookie status and the expectation that new SEALs needed to "earn their stripes" before offering opinions. As his team deliberated the best approach and devised their plan, Alex deliberated within himself whether to say anything, conscious that vocalizing his concern risked his being perceived as disrespectful at best and cowardly at worst.

Although most of us never stand on the edge of roaring rapids deciding whether to launch in, we've all had moments when we've silently debated whether to speak up or stay silent, whether to put ourselves "out there" or toe the line. Our fear creates the gap between thought and action, between what we know is the right thing to do and what we actually do. It takes courage to close it.

To clarify, closing your courage gap is not about "de-risking" your life or sheltering from problems—natural and human created. Rather, it's about bringing the bravest version of yourself to every situation—actively taking on tough problems, doing what is unpopular, facing storms head-on, and maybe even reshaping the broader landscape in the process.

As you become stronger at bridging the internal gap between thought and action, you'll become better at bridging the external gap between the reality you face and the future you want.

Much could be written on the topic of courage, particularly in the context of this moment in history when it seems in such short supply. Yet most people are too busy getting through their day to absorb, much less act on, an intellectual digest of a subject that's been explored since Aristotle dubbed it the "first of all virtues that guarantees all others." As a self-described "pracademic," it was a deliberate decision to write a relatively short book that distills theory and research into five actionable steps. I've synthesized these steps from a range of disciplines, including adult development, cognitive psychology, somatic coaching, and neuroleadership. My intention is to develop your mastery in the two essential dimensions of courage:

- Management of fear
- Willingness to act in its presence, amid real or perceived risks

If you are fortunate to live in a country that values democratic freedom, the biggest obstacle to a more meaningful life is not external. Rather, it lies in your undeveloped courage that constricts your personal freedom to act. As such, the greatest threat to our future is not our ignorance of what needs to be done; it is our unwillingness to act upon what we already know. Similarly, the greatest danger to humanity in the twenty-first century is not generative AI or climate change or foreign adversaries, it is our own lack of courage. At times, even cowardice.

> The greatest limit to your future is not that you do not know what you should do. Rather, it is that you are not willing to do what you know.

In the spirit of breaking from norms, this book is absent of chapters. Instead, it contains this introduction, the five steps, and a conclusion that invites you to help others be braver, creating "cultures of courage" that unleash collective potential. Each step revolves around a core thematic that, when combined, form a holistic evidence-based framework (shown in figure I.1) that leverages the cognitive (Steps 1, 2, and 5), physiological (Step 3), and behavioral (Step 4) domains of behavioral change. The Courage Gap Resources

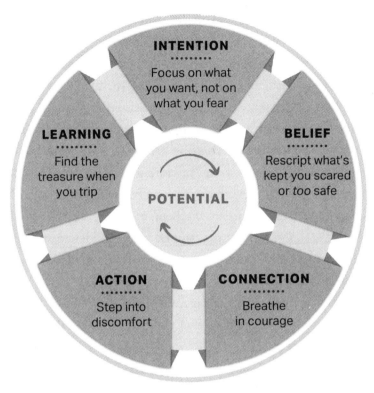

FIGURE I.1: The Courage Gap: The Five-Step Framework

section at the end of the book gives you access to the Courage Quiz and complimentary workbook. I strongly recommend you take the quiz now (it will only take a couple minutes) to assess your current courage gap and download the workbook to deepen your reflection in each step and formulate your plan to close your gap by the time you've finished it.

Step 1, Focus on What You Want, Not on What You Fear, is based on the principle that what you focus on expands. Until you decide what you value more than protecting yourself from what you don't want, fear will direct your life, often in ways beyond your conscious awareness. This step helps you identify where you've fallen into a "fear trap," reset on your North Star, and clarify your highest intention—for the challenges you're facing right now and for the ultimate enterprise of your life.

Step 2, Rescript What's Kept You Scared or *Too* Safe, puts your beliefs—that is, the "stories" you're constantly telling yourself—under the microscope. By identifying where your stories—which create your "operating system" for action—have left you driving with one foot on the accelerator and the other on the brake, you can edit them. By rescripting the stories that have stoked your stress, sapped your confidence, or kept you navigating life with blind spots, a whole raft of new possibilities will emerge.

Step 3, Breathe in Courage, will help you connect to the courage *within* you and *around* you, transforming the physiology of fear into the psychology of courage. By learning to "embody courage"—in how you walk, talk, "show up" for life—you can tap the full power of your internal and external environments to amplify your influence in *every* domain. Drawing on your sharpened focus, upgraded operating system, and full presence, you're poised to step into your courage gap.

Step 4, Step into Discomfort, is where the rubber hits the road. Based on my childhood lesson that "growth and comfort can't ride the same horse," this step is where you reset your relationship with discomfort and convert your fear into a potent catalyst for action. By practicing what I call the "one-brave-minute" rule, you'll summon the courage to step forward, strengthening your neural pathways with each successive step, growing progressively more comfortable with being uncomfortable.

Finally, in Step 5, Find the Treasure When You Trip, you learn how to rise when you fall, mining the lessons failure holds to grow the wisdom needed to elevate your relationships, leadership, and whole life to a higher ground. While this step will build your resilience, it goes beyond "bouncing back" to deepening your entire experience of life itself. You will learn how to practice self-compassion, forgive your fallibility, and make peace with your "unfinished self." In doing so, you will shed any shame that's held your future captive to past hurts and failings, emboldening you to pursue the highest intention for your life, less needless angst.

> Inner development determines outer effectiveness. Your unfaced insecurity will sabotage even your best efforts.

The order of these steps is less critical than the inner work they require. In the realm of adult and leadership development, this work is often referred to as "vertical development."[4] Distinct from horizontal development—which encompasses gaining skills and knowledge to excel at *what* you do—vertical development transforms *who* you are—expanding your capacity for life and leadership itself, particularly in today's world of heightened complexity and ambiguity. My own journey of inward exploration began in my twenties: while living in Papua, New Guinea, I decided to confront a self-sabotaging pattern of disordered eating that had plagued me since adolescence.

In the same period, I was held at gunpoint in a robbery and lost my first child midpregnancy a few days later. As rocking as these experiences were, they became a catalyst for a profoundly empowering inner journey that continues to teach me how our highest growth stems from working through the layers of fear that can estrange us from the full quota of our gifts and capacity to do good for others. In the decades since, I've been privileged to work with thousands of people, from pioneering entrepreneurs to leaders entrusted with stewarding some of the world's largest organizations, even nations. These experiences have reinforced my deep belief that all lasting change extends from the inside out, and the cornerstone of leadership development lies in cultivating the person staring back from the mirror. Until we reprogram our self-protective patterns of thought and behavior, they'll undermine our decisions, impede our endeavors, and confine the good we could otherwise do. Through my work with "insecure overachievers," I've repeatedly witnessed how people rise in the ranks because of *what they do*, but cap themselves because of *who they are*. External expertise—technical, commercial, political, and so on—that isn't coupled with inner mastery ultimately generates fearful environments that leak value, stymie potential, and leave everyone less secure and worse off.

Whereas much of my work today is focused on helping people lead others more bravely (a term I use synonymously with courage), this book is focused squarely on how to better lead yourself. It's my hope that it will embolden braver leadership at the highest tables to elevate the quality of decisions and move organizations, communities, countries, and humanity forward. Yet I did not write it just for people with formal leadership authority. I wrote it for anyone who wants to lead their most authentic life. As such, I define a leader as anyone with the courage to act as one for the higher good.

In recent years, I've had the opportunity to support leaders in weak and burgeoning democracies and some who have been exiled from oppressive regimes like Iran, Myanmar, and Afghanistan. As gut-wrenching as some of their stories have been, they've also galvanized my conviction that creating a better world requires creating a braver world, and creating a braver world begins with becoming the bravest version of ourselves—looking within and examining where fear is keeping us from taking the very actions that would serve us and lift others.

The future will be fraught with difficulty, but it will also be brimming with opportunities. Only those who have developed their courage will be able to seize them. So if ever there was a time to heed the call to courage in your life, *it is now*.

Sometimes your call to courage will be to take the less secure or more unpopular path.

Sometimes your call to courage will compel you to vocalize what many think but fear to say.

Other times it will be to extend an apology, turn down a sought-after opportunity, or seek common ground for the common good.

At *all* times, it will require taking 100 percent responsibility for your experience of life, however unwanted or unfair the circumstances.

Having survived the evil of the Nazi concentration camps that killed his wife and parents, Viktor E. Frankl concluded that "between stimulus and response there is a space. In that space is our power to choose our response. In our response lies our growth and our freedom."[5] Nothing robs our freedom more swiftly than fear. Nothing expands our freedom more profoundly than courage.

I know you sometimes wrestle with fear. But I also know your courage. It's my hope that you will come to discover the power and freedom that Frankl spoke of, because the greatest reward for stepping into your courage gap is not *what* you accomplish. It's *who* you become.

Closing your courage gap is not a short course but a lifelong endeavor. It will stretch you in new ways and humble you in others. At times, your deeply etched instinct for looking good and feeling secure will win out over doing good and forging change. Yet as with every worthwhile journey, it will eventually lead you home . . . to the deepest part of yourself and, some distant day, to knowing, *really* knowing at a soul-deep level, how little reason you ever had to be afraid.

"We must meet the time as it seeks us," wrote Shakespeare.

This time is seeking you.

Let us begin.

STEP 1

INTENTION

Focus on What You Want, Not on What You Fear

I n my midtwenties, I landed a great job. For someone my age, it had solid cachet. I'd be attending VIP events. Meeting important people. On paper, I'd hit the jackpot, particularly for a girl who'd not long since left life on a dairy farm.

My little happy dance lasted about two weeks.

By week three I started to realize that I'd joined a dysfunctional team, with a disengaged manager and disgruntled coworkers who promptly decided to take out their unhappiness with life on me. The fact that I'd been hired into a more senior role than them, despite being several years younger and less experienced, clearly fueled their resentment.

I could have asked my manager for more direction.

I could have talked to the department head and sought his guidance.

I could have confronted my coworkers' snide remarks and bullying behavior.

But I didn't.

Sure, I did my job. Made some friends. Met some interesting people. Yet over time I grew increasingly miserable and disengaged. My lunch breaks grew longer. My working days got shorter. Within a year, I decided to leave.

On my final day, I was asked to meet the divisional director. "I'd hoped you'd have a big future here, Margie," he said from behind his mahogany desk in his plush corner office. Figuring I had little to lose at this point, I spoke truthfully. The promises broken. The lack of direction. The "mean girls." He frowned. "I wish I'd known," he replied, sounding genuinely disappointed. "If you'd come to me, I could have done something."

But I hadn't. Not because I didn't think it might have been helpful, but because I simply lacked the courage. It all felt too uncomfortable, too awkward, too scary. And so I let my fear of an uncomfortable conversation keep me from doing something, *anything*, to improve my situation. Instead, I shrunk back. I settled. I languished. And after a year, I left.

Might things have improved had I spoken up? Maybe. Might I have even risen in the ranks? Who knows. Within a few months, I'd packed up my life to pursue an adventure beyond Australia's shores. However, even though I failed the test of courage in that short chapter of my early career, I didn't fail to learn the lesson.

Whenever fear governs our decisions, it makes us an accomplice in our problems as well as their victim, perpetuating our problems and shortchanging our future. So the first step in closing your courage gap is to decide what it is that you want more than what you fear. What do you want to experience in your life? What do you want in your career, your relationships, your leadership . . . *your life?* What values do you want to define the kind of person you want to be? Until you make these decisions, every other decision and corresponding behavior will be automatically directed by your fear of what you *don't* want—leaving you permanently living under the *effect* of your circumstances rather than being the *cause* in improving them.

> Your focus on a positive outcome must exceed your fear of a negative outcome.

Until you're clear on what you most want, fear of what you don't want will pull its invisible strings. When I was in my midtwenties, I was yet to connect to what I wanted more than what I feared—and so my fear governed.

Doom headlines garner the most clicks for a reason.[1] Our brains are programmed to focus on deficits and mentally dress-rehearse the outcomes we don't want. Unless you're directing your attention to what you *do* want or *can* do, it will default to negative spaces—dwelling on what you *don't* want, *don't* have, *can't* do, or *might lose.* What's more, what you focus on expands—for better or worse, for braver or more uptight, for more confidence or self-doubt.

Try this thought experiment to see for yourself: set the timer on your phone to three minutes then start writing a list of all that you *don't* like about your life and *don't* want to happen. Notice any subtle shifts in your emotional state when your timer reaches three minutes. Then set it again but this time, list everything that is good in your life and what you'd love to happen. Again, notice the shifts in how you feel three minutes along. What does that tell you about the power of your focus?

It's a natural law that energy—expressed in your creativity, ingenuity, and inventiveness—flows where your attention goes. The more you focus on the negatives, the more mental real estate they occupy, magnifying your perception of danger and amplifying negative emotions to the point that you end up living in the very reality that you want to avoid, anxious about potential situations that might never actually occur. Dwelling on deficits also closes down your ability to identify novel solutions. Metaphorically and literally. Researchers have found that when we focus on negatives, our peripheral vision narrows,[2] literally restricting what we can see and confining our actions to a smaller range of options than actually exists.

On the flip side, when you focus on what you *do* want, you elevate your vantage point and ignite your creativity. Suddenly you can connect dots, spot opportunities, and see relationships not readily obvious to others, bringing your full creative resources to the moment at hand. Focusing on the positive outcomes you want taps latent energy that enables you to show up with the "can-do" spirit that attracts like-minded people and opportunities to advance. If you're still remotely cynical, here is another simple experiment: for the next twenty-four hours, focus your attention and conversations solely on what you want and what you can do. No complaining. Then notice the shifts in your emotional state. You can thank me later.

> What you focus on expands.
> Focusing on what you're afraid
> might happen leaves you living in
> the very reality you don't want.

In 1978, President Jimmy Carter brought Anwar Sadat and Menachem Begin, leaders of Egypt and Israel, to Camp David with the intention of ending the long conflict between their countries. Although many were skeptical that any semblance of agreement could be reached, Carter was determined to spare the loss of more lives and forge a pathway toward peace. Day after day, night after night, he would walk back and forth between their lodgings, sometimes until three or four in the morning. His commitment to finding common ground for common good eventually culminated in the historic Camp David Accords. As difficult as it may be to imagine enduring peace across the Middle East right now, the truth remains that all it takes to end the cycles of conflict that create so much human suffering is for leaders to prioritize the pursuit of peace over the desire to win war, consolidate power, or seek retribution. Overcoming human nature is no small endeavor, but it is the enduring hallmark of the most noble.

Similarly, Orville and Wilbur Wright didn't get a heavy machine airborne by focusing on the law of gravitational pull but by harnessing the aerodynamic forces of flight. Likewise, you too will fly higher when you focus on what you want—what you *really* want—not on what you don't.

Focus on what you are *for*, not on what you're against.

Focus on forging *new ground*, not on protecting what you have.

Focus on *possibilities* to improve the future, not on ruminating over past failures.

Focus on doing more of what *energizes* you, not on dwelling on what pulls you down.

Focus on *optimizing* the resources you have, not on complaining that you don't have enough.

Focus on what you'd love to *create* by the end of the week/year/your life, not on how hard it will be.

Focus on being more of the person you'd love to work/live/hang out with, not on avoiding disapproval.

> The fearful mind creates the gap. The brave heart closes it.

If you're not sure what you really want, you're not alone. Most people spend more time planning their next vacation than how they'll spend their life. Yet, if we have no North Star to align short-term decisions with long-term aspirations, what will make us feel better *right now* will overshadow what will fulfill us most. It's why so many people spend precious energy in a hive of activity—chasing and striving, reacting and impressing—yet live on a carousel going in circles. As GPS technology has found by tracking people's movements, in the absence of a clear landmark we naturally walk in circles.[3]

Roman philosopher Cicero coined the phrase *summum bonum*— Latin for "the highest good"—believing that it was everyone's duty to aspire to the highest good. Although this can be done in any context—in your relationships, family, team, company, community, or country—there is no greater context than the highest good that you want for your life. After all, you don't get a second shot at it.

My mum was eighty-four when she passed away. A "solid innings" by some measures, but gone too soon by my own. I've thought about life a lot since she died. And about death, including my own. Perhaps the most valuable gift of death lies in how it sharpens our appreciation for the gift of life. In grieving for Mum, I've returned to the same deep knowing I felt after mourning the death of my brother Peter, who took his life after his long and torturous struggle with schizophrenia.[4] That is, I want to live my life in a way that honors the gift of life itself, the life Peter never got to live, using my talents to help others use their own for the *summum bonum*.

The life we most aspire to live will often require sacrificing what is comfortable now for what will serve our highest good later. Whenever our decisions are directed by short-term gratification or insecurity alleviation—proving our significance, touching up our appearance, or avoiding criticism—we risk our entire life being consumed by impression management and outcompeting the Joneses. To paraphrase D. H. Lawrence, we are not happy when we are doing just as we want, but when we are doing what our "deepest self" wants.[5]

What does your *deepest self* want? As Lawrence also pointed out, uncovering what our deepest self truly desires can take some digging. What I know from my own inward exploration is that when I'm connected to my true self—to what I believe is the sacred within each of us, which I call God, and which knows beyond what my intellect ever can—the answer becomes clear, even if it evokes fear in some form.

In early October 2001, a few weeks after 9/11, I boarded a flight in Australia with Andrew, our eight-week-old baby, two-year-old, and three-year-old to move to Dallas, Texas. Five planes. Thirty-six hours. A marathon trip with young kids made even longer from the impact September 11 had on air travel. For the next three months, we lived out of suitcases awaiting our belongings. I had no social support and felt as though I'd landed on Mars; every day felt like another long and tiring marathon. Soon after we'd unpacked the last box in our rental home, my body sent me a thousand mini stop signs in the form of head-to-toe psoriasis. Not only did I feel down—on myself; on my spots; on Andrew, whose job had bought us to a place where I wondered if I'd ever fit in—but each time I glanced in a mirror, I realized I was far vainer than I wanted to think.

When Mum's cousin offered to fly from California to "hold the fort" so that Andrew and I could get away for a few days, it was an easy yes. Lying on a beach a month later, I did a guided meditation to imagine the highest vision for my life ten years out. I quickly saw myself forging a whole new path coaching and empowering people. A nanosecond later, another image flashed to the foreground. It was me and what . . . wait . . . *four* children! *What?!* That can't be right? Four is one human more than three. *God, can you not see these spots?!!*

Fear dialed up my self-doubt to max volume. *How on earth can you manage four kids with no family nearby AND have a career? Who the hell do you think you are!?* Yet I knew the vision wouldn't have been imprinted on my heart if I wasn't capable of raising four children and honoring a call beyond my family. While my mind shouted a million reasons why not, my heart knew I'd be selling myself short if I allowed my fear—of falling short as mother or coping with the inevitable ball-~~juggling~~dropping act—to call the shots. Sometimes our heart knows the path we must take well before our head is ready to surrender resistance.

What does your *deepest self* want? What future state ignites a spark in you, making you feel more alive, even as your fears waste no time in filling the gap between that future and where you currently stand? The bolder your vision, the more likely they will.

Your longing to live a deeply rewarding life will often be at odds with your desire to live a secure one. This is why so many sacrifice their passion and potential on the illusive altar of security. It's also why pursuing your highest good will never be wholly comfortable. More often, that pursuit will call on you to do the very things that your insecure, comfort-loving, cautious self would prefer you didn't. Surrendering control.

Risking exposure. Stepping into uncertainty. True security against the risks and ravages of life cannot be found in material form.

> Be careful not to sacrifice your most rewarding life on the altar of false security.

There's no arguing that fear's directive spares you stress . . . in the short term. No risking rejection. No ruffling of feathers. No rocking of boats. No extra balls to juggle and drop. (Though on that matter, my kids improved their eye-hand coordination picking up my dropped balls and throwing them at each other.) Yet just because something is hard doesn't mean it's bad. Your greatest source of stress will never come from hard work or courageous action, but from the lack of it:

- From the conversations you did *not* have
- From the boundary you did *not* firmly set
- From the request that you did *not* clearly make
- From the feedback you did *not* give and accountability you did *not* manage
- From the tension you did *not* address
- From the change you did *not* make . . . or not make soon enough

The brave thing you most need to do is often far more mundane than changing career or launching a startup. More often it's something far simpler. Making a phone call instead of texting. Saying no to an invitation knowing you will likely disappoint. Asking for help or delegating a task rather than doing it all yourself. Admitting "I don't" when feeling pressured to pretend that you do. Saying sorry. Saying "Enough!" Saying "I do." To quote psychologist Carl Jung: "Where your fear is, there is your task."[6]

The smarter we think we are, the more cunningly our fears work in the background. Working with insecure overachievers has taught me that fear has many faces and only occasionally expresses itself in overt knee-shaking trepidation. More often it hides behind intellectualized emotions, a false sense of urgency, being hyper-controlling, or constant posturing and name-dropping. Or, on the other side of the behavioral spectrum, being overly accommodating, excessively humble, or *too* nice for our own good or anyone else's.

Fear is at the wheel anytime our desire to prove, please, or impress matters more than serving the higher good over the longer haul. Whenever we bifurcate our public and private personas, when we procrastinate on addressing tension in a relationship, or relentlessly pursue "success" or avoid situations where we risk being exposed as "less than" on some measure, fear is at play. If you haven't spent time identifying what makes you feel vulnerable, your decisions will be governed by avoiding it.

Neuroimaging technology has enabled a deeper understanding of how fear is embedded in the neural operating system of our psyche. By identifying which parts of the brain light up when making decisions, we know that the reward centers of our brain are twice as sensitive to potential

loss—of approval, status, money, reputation, power, pride—
as they are to potential gain. Our default programming is to
protect against what we *don't* want rather than pursuing what
we *do* want. To say this another way, we put more value on
not losing $100 than on gaining $100. One study asked people
to walk seven thousand steps a day for six months. Some were
paid $1.40 for each day they achieved the goal; others lost $1.40
each day they failed to walk. The second group hit their target
50 percent more often.[7] As Daniel Kahneman wrote in *Thinking, Fast and Slow*, "We hate to lose more than we love to win."[8]

> Through facing your deepest fears
> you reclaim your greatest power.

Our brains are extraordinarily complex and some very
"brainy" people like Kahneman have written much to help us
understand them better. Kahneman refers to the two parallel
neural circuits driving the operating system enabling you to
read this book as our fast and our slow brain. Our fast brain
engages one of the more primitive parts of our brain, known
as the amygdala—sometimes labeled as the "monkey brain."
Automatic, impulsive, intuitive, and error-prone, the amygdala governs much of how we think and what do in our everyday lives. If you've ever jumped out of the way as an electric
scooter sped toward you on a sidewalk, you have your fast
brain to thank. Likewise, anytime you've overreacted or been
impulsive—saying or doing something before your rational
"slow" brain kicked into gear—you can point to your fast

brain, which generates emotions without the participation of consciousness, spurring you to react to perceived threat before you're even fully conscious of exactly what is happening. To be clear, your slow brain isn't actually slow. Rather, it requires mental exertion to deliberately reason and make more complex decisions.

Clearly, we wouldn't enjoy the lives we have today if not for the brilliant gray matter between our ears. The problem is that unlike the technology which scans that matter and runs our lives, our Stone Age brains haven't evolved much in sixty thousand years. This makes our fast brain prone to assess a situation as life-or-death even when our life is not remotely at risk. As neuroscientists have found, our emotional responses to psychological injury—such as feeling humiliated in a meeting, socially excluded, professionally marginalized—use the same neural circuits as a physical injury.[9] The sources of our anxiety are rarely legitimate threats to our life but more often threats to our sense of significance. Only occasionally are they wholly rational.

This story, ripped from the pages of my own life, is an example. A prolonged drought forced my dad to sell his herd of dairy cows. As the cattle truck pulled out from the loading dock, it suddenly occurred to me that it was driving away with our family's sole source of income. Looking up at Dad as he watched that truck move slowly down our gravel lane, I asked him: "How will we get money now, Dad?" He wrapped his arm around me and replied, "I don't know, Margie." Then, squeezing my shoulder to reassure me as much as himself, he added: "We have to trust that the Good Lord will provide." My nine-year-old brain tried to imagine how the Good Lord would do this. Would we win the lottery? Would a bag of money just show up on the back verandah?

> Be led by your values, not your emotions. When your values are clear, courage becomes easier.

Neither happened. Rather, Dad spent the next four years doing contract labor, fixing fences, baling hay, and building vacation rental cabins by the lake nearby. We lived in hand-me-down clothes and never dined out (ever). Our Friday-night tradition of ordering fish'n'chips never actually included fish. It was too expensive. However, we had plenty of eggs from our chickens and meat from our remaining few cows and pigs, and we regularly ate freshly caught fish bartered with the local fisherman for milk. And of course, a boundless supply of milk—full cream, unpasteurized, unhomogenized, straight from the udder to our cereal bowl. Yet although we never went hungry, for many years a deeply etched fear of ever again feeling "poor" would highjack my rational brain and trigger scarcity thinking that left me focused on what I feared to lose rather than on what I wanted to gain, to give, to create or enjoy. More on this in the next step.

As different as your childhood likely was from mine, most of us carry psychological scar tissue from our childhood into our adult lives that pulls our attention toward what we don't want to reexperience, regardless of how irrational that fear may be in the context of our lives today. Working through the experiences that our developing brain processed as "near-death" in our childhood (regardless of whether they actually were) is the work of every flourishing adult.

This isn't about wishing fear away. That would be to wish away what has secured the human species from extinction. It's just that in today's world, we aren't staring into a campfire under the stars, slingshot at hand, ears tuned for predators. Rather, we are staring into our screens over a triple-skim venti Frappuccino, scrolling newsfeeds with algorithms engineered to stoke insecurity. So the goal is not fear extermination but fear regulation. Learning to recognize these four common cognitive distortions that magnify fear and contract courage—I call them "fear traps"—will help you do just that:

- Discounting the future
- Fearcasting worst-case scenarios
- Rationalizing inaction and excess caution
- Betraying yourself to secure status with others

Beware of discounting the future

If you've ever agreed to do something months in advance only for that distant day to arrive and regret ever saying yes, you've fallen into the first fear trap of valuing the future more cheaply than the present. The fact that for 98 percent of human history, people didn't live beyond thirty-five, leaving little future to be concerned about, may explain why we value the emotions we'll feel in five minutes' time far more than those we'll feel in five weeks, much less five years.

Yet this temporal bias that makes you prone to discount

the future can drive you to procrastinate doing the very thing you know would serve you most. Like putting off making a change, or taking a chance or declining an invitation to avoid the momentary awkwardness of disappointing someone only to feel more disappointed and frustrated with yourself later on. Every day you stick with something that is not moving you toward what you most want is a day you're not investing in what could.

Reel in fearcasting worst-case scenarios

Anxiety stems from an anxious thought about an unwanted future state. The more uncertainty we face, the more prone we are to fill the void with "dread images"—*I'll end up destitute, my family will disown me*—turning our forecasts into fearcasts. In the process, we often scare ourselves more with our imagination than reality ever does.

Prior to my first book *Find Your Courage* coming out, a vivid nightmare woke me from my sleep. Plastered in my mind's eye was the front page of the *New York Times* with a photo of me (which looked more like a mug shot) consuming the entire cover. Above it was a single headline: "World's Worst Author." Intellectually I knew that even if I had managed to write the world's worst book, no newspaper would waste its column inches on it. More famous for its potency than for its logic, fear makes us maestros at creating horror movies in our heads that would give Stephen King a run for his money. To change the channel on your self-directed horror movie, ask yourself: *What is true right now? What do I want to be true in the future?* Focus your energy on that.

Stop rationalizing inaction and excess caution

Our brains are also little Einsteins at rationalization, quickly able to reel off 101 reasons to run for the hills, toe the line, or play it totally safe even as our deepest self urges otherwise. *I'm too young, too busy, too old, too inexperienced. It's winter. It's summer. It's Tuesday. Besides, no one else is saying anything!* If you're looking for an excuse not to do what feels right and true for you, you'll always find it. But be honest with yourself: what is your excuse costing you? What if the exact opposite were true: What if this were actually the perfect moment to speak up or step forward? Only by confronting the cost of the excuses that keep you yielding to fear can you unlock latent courage.

Avoid betraying yourself to secure status with others

Long before selfie culture, we humans have sought to ensure that our "stock" is rising in the eyes of our "pack," or to at least ensure that it's not falling. Wired for belonging, we like making a positive impression and feeling like we belong. Yet even if you've never touched up a photo before posting it online, you've probably still had moments when you've put more weight onto the opinions others have about you than you have on the opinion you've had of yourself. Given that social distress is neurologically indistinguishable from physical pain, it makes sense that the thought of losing status—with peers or among friends—can swiftly activate a self-protective instinct. And in a digital world where algorithms engineered to stoke social insecurity are seven thousand generations ahead of our neural circuitry, that instinct can be triggered often.

Whenever you're moving toward a deepening of yourself, the superficiality of the world will try to pull you back into the shallows of impression management. The good you do and fulfillment you seek will expand in direct proportion to your willingness to risk looking bad—to feeling rejection, ruffling feathers, embarrassing yourself, disappointing others, or falling short. Which brings us full circle . . .

In what direction is your deepest self calling you to move in the days and months ahead? If your courage held the paintbrush, what picture would it paint on the canvas of your life? What vision for your future ignites purpose and passion and excitement within you? It doesn't have to raise eyebrows or win accolades. You don't have to aspire to climb a mountain or into the C-suite. What does matter is that it inspires *you*— even if it scares you. The best visions always will.

> Be before do. Grounding yourself in the certainty of who you want to *be* elevates what you *do*.

The vision for your life holds power. It galvanizes your purpose and marshals your courage and puts you on a whole new footing and higher trajectory. And even if you should fall short of achieving it, you still grow into a bigger version of yourself for daring to try. So if your path looks harder, it's because your calling is higher. Rather than interpret trepidation as a sign that you can't move forward, view it as a signal that you're headed in the right direction. Any aspiration that isn't stretching you, isn't worthy of you.

Dale was on the vestry for his church, whose congregation had been declining year after year for over a decade. While I knew nothing about his church, knowing that all things rise and fall with leadership indicated there was a gap between its required and current leadership. When I asked Dale what conversations he'd had with his pastor, he quickly explained that his pastor had a "strong personality" and could be very defensive. So Dale had tiptoed lightly around the elephant in the room, making the occasional suggestion while trying to secure the church's financial position. "What kind of steward do you want to be?" I asked him. "Faithful," he replied. "A man of honor and integrity." Then I asked him what conversations a person who was faithful would have. Immediately his expression conveyed the realization that he needed to risk discord to stay in integrity with himself. Spiritual maturity requires emotional maturity. Conceding an inch of your truth to keep false peace betrays the person you want to become and the good you might otherwise do. While the desire to "look good" runs deep, if we aren't mindful, our fear of looking bad will limit us from doing good.

When you are clear about *who* you want to be, it will embolden you to do the very thing you might otherwise shy away from. We often overestimate the stress of taking brave action and underestimate the cumulative stress of cautious inaction. This is as true in business as it is in our personal lives. One study found that people often misjudged the stress they anticipated from having a deeper conversation, reporting

31

afterward that they felt less vulnerable than they had initially expected.[10] So if you feel anxious at the thought of taking brave action such as an awkward conversation, know that any stress you feel now will ultimately pale in comparison to the cumulative angst you will experience if you fail to act.

Given that you're reading this book, I'm assuming that you want to be a courageous person and a braver leader in your own way. This may sound somewhat trivial, but deciding who you want to be—for yourself, those people you love, and those you lead—is one of the most significant decisions you will ever make. Because once you've decided who you want to *be*, you'll become clearer about what you need to *do*. Research bears this out. According to James March's identity model of decision making, when we're making a decision, we automatically ask ourselves these questions:

- What kind of person am I?
- What kind of situation is this?
- What would a person like me do in a situation like this?[11]

Abraham Lincoln said that "it often requires more courage to dare to do right than to fear to do wrong."[12] You are as courageous as you choose to be in any given moment. Each day that you decide who you will be—regardless of how others are behaving or how daunting your challenges—is a day you empower yourself to meet those challenges better. As Stanford researchers found, when we ground ourselves in the "self-certainty" of who it is we are certain that we want to be, it helps us to show up that way in situations that can otherwise trigger us to shrink down, play it too safe, respond defensively, or over aggressively.[13]

> The quality of your life will increase
> in proportion to the courage you
> bring to every decision.

The biggest barrier standing between you and your most inspiring life and legacy is not external. It's you. Dismantling that barrier begins with deciding to focus on what you want—on your boldest vision and highest good. While life may throw a few curve balls your way, the decisions *in* your life, not the conditions *of* your life, are what will ultimately shape the person you become. As Richard Boyatzis, renowned for his work in self-directed leadership, wrote: "While there will always be much outside our sphere of immediate control, who we choose to become is very much within our power to create."[14]

"I always wanted to be somebody," said comedian Lily Tomlin. "I should have been more specific."[15] In that job early in my career, I had yet to decide who I wanted to be, so my fear ruled. Had I decided, I'd have felt compelled to speak up. And even if doing so didn't change the outcome, I'd still have grown a little in my own estimation. As it was, I shrunk a little instead. It took several years of deep inner work to decide who I wanted to be.

What about you? Whatever caused you to pick up this book, first decide the kind of person—partner, colleague, leader, parent, friend—you want to see when you look in the mirror. Write down who it is you want to be. Crystallize it. Commit to it. Post it on your fridge. Share it with a friend. Send me an email! Let the virtues and values that call you to being the best version of your self become your ultimate North Star. When you're clear about who you want to be, it helps you close the gap on what you are presently doing and what you need to do.

> Courage is a decision,
> not a feeling.

Decide that your commitment to what you most want— to the bravest vision for your life and the values that underpin it—is more important to you than avoiding what you *don't* want. Because in the end, what matters more than anything you achieve is who you become.

I'm excited about who you are becoming. I hope we'll meet one day.

Now let's get to work on rescripting your story that's kept you scared, stuck, or living a smaller life than serves you or anyone else.

STEP 2

Rescript What's Kept You Scared or *Too* Safe

We human beings are story-making machines. I'm not saying we're all born to pen the next Harry Potter series, but rather that we're neurobiologically wired for creating stories—a catch-all term for the beliefs, assumptions, labels, and "rules" that reflect our perception of reality. Dating back to when our ancestors carved and painted their stories onto cave walls, people have told stories to make sense of themselves and the world. Among all life forms, we stand apart in our ability to continually construct narratives about ourselves and our lives. You're likely creating one right now.

About this book. About me. About what all of this has got to do with you being braver.

In short: plenty.

Your stories are either serving you—closing the gap between the life you have and the life you want, widening your options for action, and building your courage to take those actions—*or they're not.* In which case, they're confining you, leaving fear to push the pen across the pages of your life.

This step will help you become a better storyteller. Not so you can be a more entertaining raconteur at dinner parties (as wonderful as that would be) but so you can break out of the box your stories have inadvertently confined you into.

Before you can edit your story, you must identify it. This is a little trickier than it sounds. Just as fish don't know they're in water, we often can't see our stories. This is because our brain is always working hard to justify stories that make us feel safe, certain, or superior, even if, over time, they're leaving us stuck, shortchanging our future and selling out on the person staring at us in the mirror.

We unconsciously craft self-protective stories that shield us from uncomfortable truths. Whenever someone's identity rests heavily on a story they've fabricated from selective threads of evidence, any suggestion that their story has some holes in it can feel like a threat to their entire being. So they double down on their rightness, dismissing any contradictory facts that fracture the world as they've constructed it. You've likely met a few people who've woven themselves a story that hems them into a straitjacket of their own making, entrapped by their own ego-protecting narrative.

I can never . . . make that change, handle that pressure, start over, reach the C-suite, build the business . . .

I'm just too . . . old, young, sensitive, emotional, insecure, shy, lazy, perfectionistic . . .

I can't just go and . . . confront my boss, relocate my family, walk away . . .

Those people are all . . . impossible, deplorable, idiots, heartless, barking mad . . .

We're programmed to believe that how we see the world is how it is. But you don't see the world as it is but as *you are*, through a lens tinted by your experiences—particularly the most painful. Even the most ardent truth seekers among us can succumb to false perceptions—of themselves, of others, of dangers and opportunities—based on selective facts, half-truths, and faulty math.

Beware the certainty of your rightness. You don't know what you're wrong about.

When asked what it takes to be a great writer, Ernest Hemingway replied, "a built-in shock-proof crap detector."[1] Now I don't mean to imply that you "talk crap"—at least not knowingly. But I'll hazard a guess that not everything you tell yourself, or others, would pass Hemingway's detector test. Not because you're intending to mislead but because the easiest person to deceive is yourself.

As Nassim Nicholas Taleb wrote in *The Black Swan*, we're all subject to the "narrative fallacy" that makes us think we understand the world more than we actually do.[2] So before you attempt to rescript your story, dial your curiosity up to 10/10 and be open to the possibility that some of what you're certain you're right about may not be wholly true and might even contain some "vital lies"—the soothing mistruths we tell ourselves that reinforce the certainty of our rightness, abrogate us of responsibility (sometimes fueling a victim mindset), rationalize our choices, and airbrush messy truths.[3]

Chances are that you, like me, like to think that your take on the world is the right one. And let's face it, feeling certain in your own rightness gives a nice fuzzy, warm-in-the-belly feeling. In fact, neuroscientists have found that the emotion of certainty is no different than any other emotion, like sadness or love. And like all emotions, certainty doesn't require logic to attach to a belief. Yet our bias for certainty can blind us to alternative perspectives and contradictory evidence as you've likely witnessed when talking to people about their favorite sporting team or who they're voting for (if you dare to discuss at all!). As Daniel Kahneman observed, we often have "an excessive confidence in what we believe we know."[4] We tend to assume that our opinion is more credible than that of others, regardless of the credibility of the respective evidence,[5] and we don't adjust how confident we feel about our judgments to match the reliability of the evidence they're based upon.[6] Just because a social media influencer said it's true, doesn't mean it is.

. . . .

This brings us back to Alex and the confidence his SEAL team had in their ability to take on the extreme whitewater of Guri. As an elite group of highly trained warriors who'd spent their career operating in the most intensely hostile and high-risk environments on the planet, the SEALs were confident that they could navigate the dangers they were about to enter. Although Alex had concerns about the risks, he figured that if his far more seasoned and senior fellow SEALs thought that it was a good idea to proceed with their mission, who was he to suggest that it wasn't? In that moment, he was more afraid of not being accepted as a special forces operator than of the treacherous waters awaiting them.

As the team launched into the river, they were immediately engulfed by a cauldron of whitewater, capsizing their raft. As it submerged, they were thrust into the midst of a violent, raging current, just upriver from its most perilous stretch, armed only with their life jackets and survival instincts. The extreme conditions surpassed anything they'd faced before, including Alex. As the most dangerous section of the river approached, they were forced to draw on every ounce of skill to avoid being dragged under the wild and unforgiving rapids.

At the bottom of the rapids, Alex and three of his fellow SEALs emerged—shaken, breathless, but alive. They immediately started searching for their fifth teammate, Jason—at first assuming, then desperately hoping, that he had emerged farther downriver beyond their line of sight. As the hours passed, their search grew more desperate, and their hope dimmed. It would be three long days of searching with the help of a helicopter they called in before Jason's lifeless body was found twenty miles downstream. He had been scheduled to leave the SEALs and attend college in six months. Alex was the last person to see him alive and the first to see him dead.

SEALs are renowned for their courage for good reason. Yet even these extraordinary soldiers trained in braving immense physical danger are not invulnerable to fear—of appearing unworthy, or weak. Although Alex's circumstances were unique, the underlying dynamic is universally human. Without sufficient self-awareness, we can all become captive to self-protective stories that reinforce our desired social identity and rationalize decisions that minimize the risk of losing status with those we want to impress. This deficit of awareness makes us blind to how the story we've spun may be making us—and others—more vulnerable to greater threats.

> Facing the truth without diluting it down is your admission price to genuine freedom.

As you read this, you may be thinking, *Oh boy, So-and-So needs to read this! They're totally blind to their blindness!* Maybe so. But consider that maybe not everything you've been telling yourself is true either.

It takes courage to examine our beliefs, to pierce the layers of self-deception that accumulate over time and admit that maybe we have been spinning a story that is not wholly true. Yet this is the brave "inner work" that shapes outer effectiveness and genuine success. As the author of your life, you can write a new story about it at any moment you choose. Your inner narrative creates your outer form. For finding solutions or prolonging problems. For agency or victimhood. For confidence or self-doubt. For building trust or eroding it. For leading change or reinforcing the status quo.

If you're unsure about whether your story is working for you, apply the 3P test of power, purpose, and possibility:

- **Power.** Does your story fuel your sense of agency and cast you as the central character in your life rather than as an extra in other people's?
- **Purpose.** Does your story align with your values and the vision of who you want to be and the life you want to live?
- **Possibility.** Does your story expand your options for action and the future you can create?

View this as a litmus test. If you can't answer the 3P questions with a hard yes, then no, your story is *not* working for you and may very well be working against you.

All behavior is driven by belief.

"Nothing in life is as important as you think it is, while you are thinking about it," observed Daniel Kahneman.[7] Your stories don't describe your reality, they generate it. As illustrated in figure 2.1, an event occurs in your life, and you create a story about it (sometimes outside your conscious

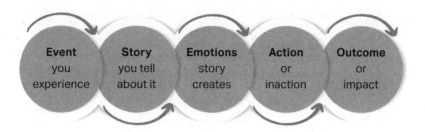

FIGURE 2.1: The Story Cycle: You Create Your
Stories, Then Your Stories Create You.

awareness). That story generates and amplifies emotions, effectively leaving you living in the feelings of your stories. Your emotions (not your logic) drive your behaviors, which in turn produce outcomes. And on the cycle continues, creating a self-fulfilling prophesy in which you create your stories as your stories create you.

As Jim Loehr wrote in *The Power of Story*, our stories "form the only reality we will ever know in this life."[8] Hence, without our mindful awareness, the subconscious biases ingrained within us—such as the inclination to validate preconceptions, defer to authority, or fixate on potential losses—can amplify our sense of peril, ensnaring us within the confines of our self-constructed narrative web.

Fortunately, as we've evolved, so too has our capacity for conscious thought. In fact, we humans are uniquely equipped to be aware of our own consciousness. While it is commonly estimated that we are only conscious of about 5 percent of the thinking that directs our decisions,[9] even this degree of awareness can profoundly impact our lives.

You might liken your capacity for rescripting your story

to your ability to steer your car—even a slight adjustment can steer your life onto a whole new trajectory. So as you stand in the stream of your thoughts, pay attention to where fear may be covertly infiltrating your stories, making you anxious or giving you air cover for living a smaller life than your deepest self is calling you to live.

Beware of muddled math and selective facts

At every turn, you can hear people stuck in stories laced with selective facts (or outright fiction) that fuel fear and siphon agency. *It's too risky to . . . give people feedback, change my career, travel to Australia . . .* Huh. If I had a dollar for every time someone in America told me they'd love to visit Australia if not for the deadly snakes, spiders, crocs, sharks, jellyfish . . . I know, I know—it's an impressive list. However, statistics show that Americans are at least five hundred times more at risk of being killed by a gun than from all these deadly creatures Down Under combined.[10] Unsurprisingly, evidence shows that our stories are spurred by a bias toward overestimating the probability of "dread events," which more readily capture our imagination.[11]

My own false perception of risk during a trip to South America illustrates my point. While traveling in Ecuador, I ventured into the jungle and upper tributaries of the Amazon. On the first day, the local tour guide announced that our afternoon activity would be floating down the river. "But didn't you say that there are piranhas in there?" I asked, as my imagination conjured up an image of them eating my toes for afternoon tea. "Oh yes, but they won't hurt you," he said. "What?!"

I exclaimed. "Have you never watched a Bond movie?! Those lethal little fish can mulch us into fish food in five seconds flat." He laughed. Turns out piranhas really don't like eating humans. Yet this little fact would have taken all the fun/terror out of a good Bond script! Disabused of the fiction that I'd assumed was fact, I glanced at my toes and jumped into the river. I then spent an exceedingly memorable afternoon floating along on its current, emerging downstream with my feet intact.

> Your fear is real, but that does not make it rational. Indulging irrational fears breeds real ones.

Your brain will automatically and unconsciously look for evidence to validate whatever story you've been telling yourself. The facts are meaningless until you create a story around them. It's why, in a time when we can so easily retreat to ideological bubbles, we need to double down on critical thinking. Put your story under the microscope. Actively search for evidence to disprove the narrative you've been telling. Who else has done the very thing you say can't be done? What inconvenient fact messes with the story you've been spinning? What is the kernel of truth in the opinion of someone who sees things diametrically different to you? Invest time to hear out those with whom you strongly disagree, listening with an ear to how you might be wrong.

Never cast yourself in the role of victim

Bad things happen. Every day. And at some point they'll happen to you, making you a victim of a circumstance outside your control. Yet there is a stark difference between being a victim and operating from a victim mentality. Victimization is a fact. Victimhood is a mindset, one that siphons the very agency needed to improve our situation and find the kernels for our growth and a higher good. Anytime your story fuels self-pity and lays all responsibility for the state of your life at sources outside yourself, it's keeping you small and short-changing your future.

As my brother Frank said after a motorbike accident left him with paraplegia, "There may be a thousand things I can't do anymore, but there are still five thousand I can. I want to do them all." He's well on his way. In fact he came all the way from Australia to visit me in Virginia, two flights and twenty-four hours of travel, while I was writing this book. Traveling across the world is not a light undertaking for anyone, but it requires a special brand of bravery for someone who is wheelchair bound. Yet Frank, refusing to let his disability limit him from living his life to the full, just got on with it. As we navigated the stairs in my very old four-story home, his can-do attitude brought home a deep truth for life: it is the story we tell ourselves that determines whether we are the captain of our lives or the captive of our circumstances.

Spinning a tale of woe can garner you pity and stoke a sense of significance. However, the payoff people get from casting themselves as a victim and bemoaning their lot in life cuts them off from their personal power to improve it.

Ditch dramatic language

"He's just terrifying, absolutely terrifying," said Lena, a rising leader, about Dan, her CEO. "Every time I'm around him I freeze up and fumble over my words." What Lena didn't know was that I had met Dan on a few occasions. Sure, Dan was driven to excel, but he was also very down-to-earth and extremely mindful of using the power of his position to elevate people, not intimidate them. If anything, he sometimes needed to be more direct. So why the disconnect? Because Lena's perception of Dan had little to do with Dan himself. Rather, it had everything to do with the story she'd created about him based on how she perceived herself (inferior) relative to anyone with his title. In saying he was terrifying—as distinct from saying that she found herself feeling nervous around him—she was terrorizing herself. Dan was no more than a walk-on extra in her melodrama.

Archbishop Desmond Tutu said, "Language does not just describe reality. Language creates reality."[12] Your brain is like a supercomputer, and your internal narrative is a program that you run on it. If you tell yourself, "My job, colleague, client, board . . . is a nightmare," your subconscious brain, always eavesdropping on the "talk track," interprets what it hears very literally. Likewise, when someone says, "I'll just die if it doesn't work out," they are triggering the greatest fear of all. Be careful not to create or exaggerate drama to satisfy your ego's craving for significance.

The words you speak become the house you live in. Make a habit of cross-examining the case you're making that keeps you stuck in place. If it cannot pass the 3P test, you're inadvertently making yourself complicit in perpetuating the very circumstances you are complaining or anxious about.

Stand guard on your language. Be mindful to distinguish between the source of your fear and how it is making you feel. For example, I get the heebie-jeebies in the presence of snakes. But that isn't because snakes are inherently scary (some people love snakes . . . albeit I think they're a sandwich short of a lunchbox). It's because snakes trigger fear in me. Same for people who are scared of flying in planes or public speaking or networking events. It's not the plane. It's not the audience. It's not the networking. It's what those things trigger inside them, fueled by the story they're telling themselves about it.

That's exactly what Lena came to realize, eventually conceding that Dan was not actually terrifying at all. Rather, she had been terrorizing herself. Her rescript: "Dan is an inspiring leader. I used to feel nervous around him, but now I'm just excited for what I'll learn from him." With that simple rescript, her face lit up and she sat a full inch taller—more empowered, more on purpose with fresh possibilities for her future (ticking all 3P boxes!). *Abracadabra!* It's no coincidence that the Hebrew roots of abracadabra translate as "I create as I speak." Your words wield magical power to create a new reality.

Lose the labels hemming you in

Labels are great for jam jars and poison containers, but when applied to people and problems, they often create an invisible boundary we don't allow ourselves to cross, reinforcing fears, dampening ambition, and generating self-fulfilling prophesies. Whether you label yourself shy, a perfectionist, a die-hard control freak, or "chronically hopeless" at a skill that would be valuable to learn, you're not giving yourself any option to be otherwise. This doesn't deny hard facts, innate preferences or personality traits. But who you are is more than a personality trait or any other label you might apply to yourself!

When I was growing up, my dad would affectionately call me "bumblefoot" because I was not particularly coordinated. While it was a term of endearment, I internalized that label and wove it into a story that my legs were simply not made for running. And so I never did. I hiked. I backpacked. I climbed mountains. But I never ran. And because I never ran, anytime I'd run more than a few hundred yards, I'd end up panting and say, "See, my legs aren't made for running." A self-fulfilling prophesy if ever there was one. Wind forward the clock to my late thirties when I went to a regular bootcamp, with runners, and I realized that *I could run*. I'd just never got past the first five minutes before. Wind forward the clock a little further and I signed up for my first marathon in a few months' time. In fact, I'm training for it right now, raising money for spinal injury research to help people like Frank. My point is not that I was born to break land-speed records but that the labels we apply to ourselves can keep us from doing the very things that would expand whole new possibilities for our lives.

Sometimes our labels get us off the hook from taking the brave actions that would enable us to move forward (or sign up for a marathon!) Just because you label yourself as introverted, disorganized, or shy doesn't mean you can't act otherwise. For instance, shyness is both an emotional state and a personality trait. One study of self-described shy adults found that when they intentionally sought to present themselves in a confident way, they gradually built their belief in their ability to engage in new relationships and challenges more boldly, creating a positive self-reinforcing cycle that empowered them further.[13] When you let go of your attachment to any label, you open the door to new habits and experiences you'd otherwise have convinced yourself were impossible for you.

> Stand guard on your language.
> Your stories don't only describe
> your reality, they create it.

Remember that image of a fourth child that appeared in the frame of my "ideal future"? At the time, I was living inside a story that it was just not possible to be a great mother to four kids *and* pursue a new career path. The fact that we lived across the world from any family support and I'd never met any women with four kids and a career until that point only compounded my doubts. Fortunately, Andrew was all-in on four kids (he'd probably have drawn the line at a dozen) and several friends loved me enough to refuse to buy into my self-limiting story. "You absolutely can! I know several women with four kids and amazing careers," said Janet. "You just need to get more help," encouraged Joan. Did that mean it would be easy? Heck no. But would it be possible? Of course! I just had to trust myself to figure it out, one day at a time, some days one meal at a time, and often by the seat of my pants. Rescripting my story didn't dissolve all my doubt, but it fortified my courage to defy it. A year later, a strong-spirited baby boy named Matthew Raymond arrived in the world . . . our little Texan who has now grown into a big one! The world is far better off for him being in it.

Chances are you've put a label on yourself or your situation that is simply not accurate. But the good thing about labels is that you can peel them off and create new ones.

Iceberg stories

Your brain is Teflon for good and Velcro for bad. It's why you can't remember the five thousand friendly interactions you've had with dogs, but you cannot forget that one dog that bit you. Your brain processes painful experiences differently than enjoyable ones. Only in mammals do cognition and memory interact to create the emotion of fear, which can accumulate over the course of our lives. Every experience during which we've felt unsafe, unworthy, or excluded lives on within us but is often, like an iceberg, beneath the surface of conscious awareness. And just as the unseen part of the iceberg sank the *Titanic*, so too it's your unconscious stories that can do the most damage to your relationships, sabotage your efforts, and keep you coming up against the same problems again and again. Until you've disentangled yourself from the fears that have sustained your life-limiting stories, they'll steer your life and you'll mistake it for destiny.

Just as the concentric circles within a tree trunk reflect the conditions of each passing year—be it flood, fire, or drought— our inner selves carry the raw emotions of our younger, less-developed selves. Even the old wounds that we've assumed had long ago healed can sometimes reopen and drive us to act in ways that hurt ourselves and others. It's why the story that's fueling our fear is rarely based on what we *think* we fear but on what we *link* to fear, tracing back to experiences long ago filed into the back recesses of our memory.

. . . .

Growing up in rural Georgia, Jim struggled with dyslexia that went undiagnosed. Tenacious and determined, Jim found workarounds for his learning challenges, persisting through high school to attend college. After graduating, he started working in the fashion industry, honing his natural talent for merchandising and spotting new trends. Always willing to put in the extra hours, he rose through the ranks to join the executive team, where he was increasingly interacting with his company board of directors and was being considered as a potential successor to the CEO. Yet whenever he was asked to present to the board, he became acutely self-conscious and often fumbled at the very moments he wanted most to impress them. "They're so intimidating," he told me. Like Lena, Jim couldn't think of a single instance of any director seeking to intimidate him. As he mined his experiences for the potential source of his fear, Jim recalled an afternoon in second grade when his teacher, a temporary substitute—called him to the blackboard in the front of his class to write the letter *G*. As he wrote it backward, he heard his classmates snigger. His teacher asked him to try again. Three more times he tried, three more times he failed, until the teacher shook her head and motioned Jim to return to his seat amid more sniggering. In recounting how small and stupid he felt that day, Jim traced the roots of his insecurity to the story his seven-year-old self had created of not being smart enough to stand in front of the board.

There's an adage in therapy that what makes us hysterical is historical. The word *hysterical* may be too strong a word for Jim—or for you—but any situation that triggers a response that's disproportional to the situation itself has its origins in a painful past experience. For Jim, here he was, fifty years later, standing in front of another board, his fear of being exposed as not smart enough sabotaging his efforts to communicate with the authority needed to win the board's trust and be considered as a potential CEO.

Jim isn't the only person with a wounded child whispering in their ear. It is the very situations that press your buttons the hardest that hold your greatest opportunities for growth. Pausing to tune into your inner narrative, fact-checking for "fake news" broadcasts, enables you to rescript the story your younger self created that keeps resurfacing and tripping you up.

Nearly thirty years had passed since Alex's experience in Guri when he and I met at a leadership conference where I'd been invited to moderate a fireside chat conversation with him, now the chief financial officer of Westrock, one of the world's largest packaging companies. We were to bring our respective expertise to a discussion on risk-taking and courage for finance leaders. In sharing what had shaped him as a leader, Alex recounted his painful experience as a new SEAL. In front of a packed room of business executives, he became teary sharing his deep regret of not having spoken up that day, of not trusting his own voice and of letting his fear of what he did *not* want—being perceived as an upstart who didn't know his place and rejected by the men whose approval he sought—keep him from raising his concern that could have saved the life of a brave man with a bright future.

> The payoff you get from your
> self-protective stories is never
> worth the price tag.

In the aftermath of the tragedy, Alex created a self-protective story that he had not failed the situation as much as the situation had failed him. Trapped by his shame and afraid of ever reexperiencing something so horrific, he erected a shell around himself and focused on controlling every variable. "I felt as though I was the only person I could trust to control the outcome of any situation," he said. "So I became a total command-and-control leader in an attempt to make myself invulnerable and ensure I'd never fail again." Seven difficult years would pass before Alex could confront the hard reality that the payoff he'd been getting from his story was not worth the price he was paying.

None of us are immune to spinning stories to shield ourselves from hard truths and uncomfortable emotions. Yet if your story isn't deepening your relationships and enriching your life, consider the possibility that you're suffering more from your story than from the painful situation that you created your story to avoid. As Henry David Thoreau observed, "The price of anything is the amount of life you exchange for it."[14]

Jim decided to rescript the story that kept him trying so hard to impress the board that he was doing the exact opposite. He replaced his old narrative, "The board directors are all smarter than me, and I have to prove I'm smart enough to be in the room" with "Every director has insights that can help us lift everyone in this company to new places." With that simple edit, Jim's focus and energy shifted from protecting the wounds of his younger self to bringing his full quota of brilliance to the enterprise he eventually went on to lead. Once again, *abracadabra!*

> Your best story brought you here. What new story does your bravest-self want to tell?

Your best stories brought you here, but maybe they're keeping you from elevating your life and leadership to a higher level. It takes courage to defy your doubts, but it also takes courage to challenge your certainties. So instead of proving yourself right, seek out evidence for what you could be missing or how you might be wrong. As Alex learned on the river, it's often less uncomfortable to just go along with what everyone else is thinking than to challenge the consensus. However, by playing it safe in the moment, we make ourselves more vulnerable to greater problems and perils over time.

What other narrative could you create that would expand your future and ignite your agency to reshape it? What old story (justification, grievance, and label) do you need to let go? What new possibilities would open up if you never told yourself that story again? Lastly, what new story would empower you to become the person you most want to be? Courageous stories don't deny potential dangers but they empower you to handle them better.

- Rather than saying it's daunting, call it stretching.
- Rather than saying you're scared, say you're excited.
- Rather than saying it's a failure, say it was valuable learning.
- Rather than saying you're too young or too late, say you're exactly on time!
- Rather than saying you don't know what you're doing, declare that you're excited to learn and figure it out as you go!

Think of a situation that's making you feel stuck, stressed, or anything but peaceful, positive, and empowered. Use the following as a guide to rescript the story (ideally with a pen in hand) that is keeping you from taking braver action.

The story I've been telling myself is . . . Yet this story has kept me feeling . . . and held me back from . . . The new story I am telling myself is . . . It makes me feel . . . . and inspires me to stop [old actions] and to start [new actions]. A year from now, this story will set me up to . . .

Rescripting your story won't dissolve all your fears—at least not right away—but it will create an opening for braver actions that will move your life in the direction of what you most want. So tell a story that reframes risk through the larger lens of your whole life. Tell a story that honors the person you know you have it within you to become. Tell a story that right-sizes your fear and emboldens your spirit.

This is my story:

I am wholly worthy and have all the courage I need to pursue the highest and holiest vision for my life. I haven't succeeded—yet—but I'm on my way, and I'm arms-open-wide excited for the adventure ahead.

Now, what new story will your bravest-self tell?

Write it down. Say it out loud. With conviction. I want to hear it. Truly.

STEP 3

CONNECTION

Breathe in Courage

Imagine for a moment that you are a world-class rugby player walking onto the field of a large stadium. Your eyes are drawn up to the crowded stands where spectators— maybe sixty thousand—are chanting, watching, waiting. The air is electric. The anticipation is palpable. Silence breaks over the stadium. And then your team captain bellows.

Kia rite! (Be ready!)

The moment has arrived. The hair on your arms stands alert. The Haka begins.

Over the next few minutes, a wave of power surges through your body, across your team, priming all for what's ahead. This ancient Māori war dance—a combination of chanting, foot-stamping, body slapping, and tongue protrusions—was traditionally performed in Polynesian cultures as a fierce display of tribal pride and unity before battle. It has since become a cherished tradition of New Zealand's All Blacks national rugby team—throwing the gauntlet at the opposing team to "bring it on!" while also priming players to "get in the zone" for victory.

As one of the most successful sports teams on the planet,[1] many have debated how much the Haka has contributed to the All Blacks success. While it's impossible to measure the impact of this ancient war dance, it raises the question: What can the Haka teach us about activating a deeper source of our own power? Turns out, quite a lot. And you don't need to learn the Haka to access it.

Although fear may start in the brain, it embeds itself in the body. In the face of a threat—real or perceived—fear spreads throughout the body, releasing stress hormones such as cortisol and adrenaline; elevating your heart rate; shallowing your breathing; impacting your muscles, digestion, and endocrine system. Your blood flow changes—moving away from your heart and into your limbs, priming you to punch someone in the face, run for the hills, or freeze in place. All of which are often counterproductive.

Yet the upside of knowing that fear embeds in your body is that it provides you with a target for intervention. Mounting clinical evidence points to the significant role that the physical state of your body—also known as your somatic state—plays in

58

your emotions, thoughts, behavior, and everyday interactions. Contrary to Descartes's dictum "I think, therefore I am," studies in "embodied cognition" and somatic psychology show that your brain is not your only resource for generating behavior.[2] Yes, your body reacts to your thoughts and emotions, but it's not a one-way street: not only can your psychological state—what you think and feel—impact your physical state, but your physical state can impact what you think and feel.

Embodying courage in ways that are relevant for the moment performs a dual function of activating the two core domains for building courage mentioned in the introduction:

- Managing fear in your sympathetic nervous system by resetting your "defensive self" at the ground level, liberating you from the reactivity that propagates fear
- Connecting you to sources—internal and external— to catalyze courage and take action amid your fear

In the *Biology of Belief*, Bruce Lipton likens every cell in our body to a battery.[3] Think the AAA variety. Although we can't confirm the degree of competitive edge the Haka provides—beyond raising testosterone and cortisol levels—the intense presence these athletes bring to embodying the spirit of the fearless warrior appears to dial up their battery cells to full power.

Of course, embodied courage takes many forms, depending on the situation. Sure, life sometimes requires armoring up and stepping into warrior mode, but as Alex Pease came to learn, it is neither healthy nor helpful to stay permanently armored up against the world. It took him a long time to see that in his efforts to make himself invulnerable to failure, he'd disconnected himself from other people and from his own humanity. The same is true for all of us. Whenever a defensive state becomes our default, we cut ourselves off from the vulnerability that lies at the heart of authentic connection and is the truest measure of courage. Not only that, but as Gavin de Becker wrote in *The Gift of Fear*, when we're continually on high alert, reacting to everything as an emergency or existential "life and death" threat, we deplete our ability to identify and respond constructively to far greater dangers.[4]

> The feeling body is stronger than the thinking brain. Knowing how fear embeds in your body provides a target for intervention.

The intention of embodying courage is not to become battle ready but to broaden your behavioral agility to bring your bravest presence to whatever each moment requires. This is particularly relevant when you find yourself in a situation that triggers a strong fear response. In the early days of the COVID-19 pandemic, as a virus jolted the world off its axis, I had such a moment.

I was living in Singapore at the time with one of our four children, the other three studying in the US. In mid-March, Andrew flew back in from visiting our kids in New York, bringing a cold with him. Runny nose. Scratchy voice. Mild fever. He put it down to jet lag. But two days on he wasn't any better, so we decided it would be good for him to check that he didn't have COVID. "I'll see in an hour or two," he said as he walked out the door to head to Singapore's National University Hospital—the only place we knew that could test for the virus at that time. Little did we know it would be thirty days before we saw each other again.

As Andrew set foot into the hospital entrance, red lights started flashing and an alarm rang loudly as his fever was detected. Within moments he was surrounded by people in hazmat suits, who escorted him to an isolation room. Five hours later, he sent me a text: *Tested positive. X-ray dark spot on lung. IV in arm.*

My mind whirled. At that early stage of the pandemic, he was the first person I knew to contract the virus. Within minutes my phone rang. It was Singapore's Ministry of Health. Memories of the SARS epidemic still fresh, they weren't taking chances.

Where are you?

At home.

Do not leave. No one is to leave. Not even to step out your door. A team will visit shortly.

Within an hour two people, maybe three (my memories are blurred), dressed for an Ebola ward knocked on my apartment door holding bottles of bleach and thermometers. We were to scrub our entire apartment. We were to record our temperature three times daily. They would also video-call us three times a day—to check our temperature, report any symptoms, and verify we were still in our apartment. We were not to step outside for fourteen days. If our temperature went up or we experienced *any* symptoms, we were to call immediately, and an evacuation team would be sent.

My entire being felt overwhelmed. I was anxious not only for Andrew but for my kids in the US suddenly thrust into situations they'd never imagined with their parents ten thousand miles away. While our oldest son, Lachlan, was hunkering down in his small New York apartment, Maddy and Matt found themselves without a home as their student dorms abruptly closed and Singapore shut down its borders to noncitizens like us. The family of a friend of Maddy's took her in. Upon hearing that Andrew had contracted the virus, she got tested, was found positive, and was quarantined. Because she'd been near her friend's grandmother, their whole family felt extremely anxious, and Maddy was left feeling guilty, overwhelmed, and even further from home.

Meanwhile, Matt, not quite sixteen, was couch surfing his way across America before finding refuge on a ranch in remote southern Colorado. As waves of overwhelm washed over me, I put into practice the tools I'd written about in my book *You've Got This!*. There was no irony lost on me that I'd been due to set off on a book-launch tour that same week. Talk about pressure-testing my own advice. For the record: it held up!

Clearly, in that moment, embodying courage didn't resemble Mel Gibson's Braveheart atop his steed, rallying his troops for battle. Showing up as our bravest self often looks more like the Dalai Lama than Rambo. For me in that moment, embodying courage was about remaining present in my power to respond calmly: inhaling courage, exhaling fear, and grounding—and *re*grounding—in my faith that *I've got this*, that my kids would be OK, and that Andrew would recover fully. Which he ultimately did, although he wouldn't recommend a month locked in a small quarantine room on a diet of "chicken rice" as a recovery plan.

Global pandemics aside, life will inevitably dish up moments when you hardly have time to scratch your head, much less master transcendental meditation or devise a detailed response plan. Such moments can propel an ordinary person to act in extraordinary ways that make headlines—diving into a frozen river or lifting a car many times their body weight to save another. Yet let's face it—our moments of "fast-thinking" fearlessness are usually few and far between. One study into whether courage is learnable found that only 5 percent of participants reported "operating on instinct."[5] For most of us mere mortals, there is a moment of internal struggle in which we weigh the options: *Do I charge forward or stay put? Speak up or say nothing? Make the ask or avoid rejection?* And the more stressed we feel while asking those questions, the more cognitively impaired we are in answering them and responding constructively. This is why practicing embodying courage in mundane moments sets you up to access it faster in the hairier ones.

> Inhabiting your body transforms
> the psychology of fear into the
> physiology of courage.

We experience life through our body whether we're conscious of it or not. In the hurly-burly of life, we can be so consumed with planning our next move or with second-guessing our last one that we forget to pause long enough to observe *who* we are being *right now*. In the process, we become habituated to living from the neck up, disconnected from our physical body, which enables us to accomplish all that we do.

Think of your body as the house in which you reside. When you're fully present in your physical being, you're the one in charge, and it's hard for unwanted guests to enter. Yet when you're living largely in your head, disconnected from your physical being, you are more at the mercy of your primal instincts, which are driven to avoid, numb, or bury uncomfortable emotions. Yet no emotion is buried dead; it always reemerges later, but uglier. Over time, our unprocessed fear accumulates, leaving us regularly wound up, buttoned up, hypervigilant, and moving through our days as a tangled bundle of tense muscles permanently on edge. As every therapist learns, "Our issues are in our tissues."[6] For people who've experienced trauma, this is particularly pronounced. "Research has confirmed what our patients tell us, that the self can be detached from the body and can live in a phantom existence of its own," wrote psychiatrist Bessel van der Kolk in *The Body Keeps the Score*.[7]

Your tension is inviting attention.

Ironically, the most powerful gateway to inhabiting your body and regulating fear in your nervous system is often overlooked because you automatically do it thousands of times every day without conscious thought: taking a breath!

Your breath pulls you into the present, reining in the fear that stems from thoughts of the future. It signals safety to your body, loosening the grip of pent-up anxiety and grounding you in the here and now.[8] Research shows that even five mindful breaths can reset your nervous system,[9] carving a clearing in the dense forest of our lives to respond with greater calm, creativity, and courage.

A simple body scan can help you become present in your body, enabling you to feel the subtle energy running through it, including where any derivative of fear is holding court. There are thousands of excellent body-scan meditations, but here is a simple one to try right now.

Direct your attention to your body—starting at the top of your head and moving downward—paying attention to any places where you feel tight or rigid or notice any sensation at all. Across your chest. In the pit of your belly. Tension in your jaw or throat or upper back. Fear has its favorite go-to places for each of us. When you notice a physical sensation, place your hand on that place and take the deepest breath you have all day. Let go any judgments about good or bad and simply notice your breath—inhaling courage, exhaling fear. You might find it helpful to silently count inhalations and exhalations—in (one), out (two), in (three), and so on—to give you a focus beyond your intrusive thoughts. Your breath will always bring you into the present—to the here and now— reeling in anxious thinking about a future moment that may never happen. Continue observing sensations—any coolness or warmth or tingling—as you keep breathing into the tense spots, untying fear-tangled knots, then exhaling them out, carrying them away. As you do, notice even the slightest loosening or lightening. Just don't expect to feel like a Zen monk first try. As Harvard psychologist Ronald D. Siegel advises, "As with any skill, your ability to focus and relax will improve with practice."[10]

If you have a strong bias for action, you might see little utility in pausing from your productive *doing* to connect to who you are *being*. After all, you've done pretty well for yourself. Yet as high-achieving "doers" rise in their chosen fields, their biggest barrier to growth often lies in how they show up for others. Often the outer winning veneer high-flyers feel pressure to maintain is the very barrier keeping them from moving to the next level of influence and impact. As a senior executive recently shared with me, "Fear has driven me to push hard and achieve a lot. But having the courage to slow down and bring more presence to myself, to my work, and to everyone else, is how I know I can make an even greater impact over the longer term." Closing the gap between your head and your heart, between what you're doing and who you're being, is where your greatest growth always lies.

> Stand tall. Walk tall.
> Play your tallest game.

When learning to walk, toddlers wobble at first, but they don't puff out or slouch over. It's our experiences en route to adulthood that shape how we carry ourselves through our lives. For this reason, embodying courage comes in a multitude of forms. For some people, softening their stiff posture and leaning into a deep, loving hug can be an act of courage; for others, it is turning on their camera for video calls to be fully seen; or standing tall and strong and fully occupying every inch of the space they hold. This was the case for Amy, a business owner and entrepreneur.

"I've hit that glass ceiling," she told me after failing to secure funding to expand her business, despite her strong track record. This wasn't her first time. She was feeling discouraged, riddled with doubt, and victimized. Having worked with many female executives and business owners, and done doctoral research in women's leadership, I am keenly aware of the barriers and gender biases women encounter. But Amy's slumped shoulders and demeanor signaled that her biggest barrier was not external. "I'm not so sure about that ceiling," I said. "But nothing, absolutely nothing, I do moves the needle," she replied, a little defensively. "I'm wondering if I'm just deluding myself about taking my business to the next level." Sure, she needed to reset her focus on her bold vision with a big why and to rescript her narrative that "absolutely nothing" she did would help. However, until she shifted how she was "showing up"—the disempowered and defensive presence she was bringing to every space and conversation— she'd keep being pulled right back into habitual self-defeating patterns of thought and emotion.

The legendary basketball coach John Wooden once remarked, "It's not how tall you are, but how tall you play."[11] Your posture—how you hold yourself and move through the world—is a proven way for regulating fear and activating courage. Research confirms what my mother intuitively knew when she'd admonish me as a teenager to stop slouching—posture shapes perception. That is, how you hold yourself impacts how you see and feel about yourself and your ability to improve your situation. One study positioned participants into either a confident posture (erect back, chest out) or a doubtful posture (slouched over, curved back). Researchers then asked participants to list their best and worst qualities. Those in the confident posture had a higher level of confidence in themselves.[12] Another study found that our posture directly influences the certainty we have in our own actions, emboldening us to do things we might otherwise shy away from.[13] Even an upright seated posture can boost positive emotions and ward off negative ones compared to a slumped sitting posture. So if you're reading this in a chair, sit up taller!

Your imagination is another powerful tool for playing your tallest game. After getting Amy's OK to "play with a little experiment," I asked her stand up and think of a time she'd felt really sure of herself. I did this knowing that connecting to positive experiences from the past can shift our emotional state in the present. She immediately recalled a time a few years earlier when she managed a successful product launch despite many obstacles. "I was brimming with chutzpah," she said. I asked her to show me how she'd stand if she were embodying chutzpah. She stood a little taller and widened her stance, pulled her hair back from over eyes, and lifted her chin. Then I asked her to close her eyes, put her hand on her heart, and embody the bravest version of the woman she wanted to be. She straightened her shoulders a little more and seemed to stand a full two inches taller prompting me to ask her what might now be possible if she approached her situation from this space. "What *wouldn't* be possible?!" she beamed back with a smile that conveyed authority and left no doubt of who was in charge of her future.

The courage you admire
in others also lives in you.

Research from Northwestern's Kellogg School of Management found that posture expansiveness—positioning oneself in a way that opens up the body and takes up space— activates a sense of power that generates behavioral change independent of a person's actual rank or role in an organization.[14] In fact, multiple studies have found that posture matters even more than hierarchy in making a person think, act, and be perceived in a more powerful way. In sum: how you hold yourself communicates more loudly than any words.[15]

You can also channel the courage of people you admire. Think of someone whose presence lights up a room and makes everyone feel a little brighter and stand a little taller. Tap your imagination once again: If they were to step into your shoes right now, with the challenges you face, what would they focus on? What story would they tell? How would they stand, walk, talk? Confidently. Positively. Authentically. I'm not suggesting that you try to walk around like Abraham Lincoln or Wonder Woman. Rather I want their brave spirit to remind you of your own.

Even wearing a smile signals to your brain that you are in

control of yourself when so much around you is outside your control. So too does your speech help regulate your fear and fuel confidence, especially under pressure. Stress alters our speech patterns—some people speak faster, softer, or more forcefully, whereas others withdraw. If your stress response is to race and rush, slow down and pause intentionally. If you tend to become forceful, soften your tone and invite people in. And if your pitch often gets higher, deliberately lower it down. A relaxed tone communicates—to your brain and to everyone else—that *you are* in charge.

Finally, envision yourself *working toward* a successful outcome rather than just picturing the final "podium moment."[16] While simulations are valuable for learning to regulate fear in high-stakes situations, mentally dress rehearsing yourself in action—speaking confidently and staying poised under pressure—can enhance performance in both cognitive and physical tasks, even tasks you've never actually performed.[17]

Design your life to cultivate courage, calm fear, and defy self-doubt.

While connecting with your physical presence summons courage for the moment at hand, optimizing the environment around you is critical to sustaining it. If its continually triggering fear and deflating self-belief, it will be hard going to embody courage over the longer term. Yet it is precisely because your environment is such a potent "triggering mechanism,"[18] as Marshall Goldsmith wrote in *Triggers,* that you need to be deliberate in architecting one that activates your courage and champions your highest talents and aspirations, not your deepest insecurities. If you don't design your life to empower yourself, it will hold power over you. And of all the triggers in your environment, none is more important than the people you surround yourself with.

At an event with the Women's Democracy Network—an organization I support that helps women grow political influence globally—Nicaraguan human rights activist Berta Valle said, "It is my network of relationships that helps me to be brave" in regard to her stand against the authoritarian Ortega regime. "I cannot do this by myself. I have courage because I have people around me who sustain me, who have my back, who help me find my voice." We simply cannot be brave on our own. Or not for long.

> Your connection to others
> provides the oxygen for you
> to walk taller through life.

It's through our connection with others that we grow into the bravest version of ourselves. Research in mirror neurons has proven that the people around us shape our stories, aspirations, emotions, and decision-making. "We spiritually gain strength from the guys beside us, from the ground that we stand on," said a former All Blacks player about the Haka.[19] So yes, you must breathe in courage, but it's your connectedness with others that provides the oxygen for you to walk taller through life, particularly when problems press in or you've ventured out onto the far limb and you're starting to worry that the branch will give away on you.

Surround yourself with people who bring out your best and help you think bigger. The kind who care more about you than they care about you liking everything they say. The kind who will call you out when you've spun a story that's keeping you small. The kind who are quick to celebrate your wins, however small, and reframe your losses, however large.

On the flip side, set up "courage rails" with courage crushers who tread on dreams, dwell on the potential downsides, and second guess your every move. Give them wide berth. Limit your exposure. Discern what and how much you share with them. They're not bad people; they're just not helping you grow into a better person. Wish them well. We each have our own gap to close. You've set a faster timeline.

Whenever you're leveling up your life, you must level up the systems—the habits, rituals, and structures—that support it. As James Clear wrote in *Atomic Habits*, "You don't rise to the level of your goals. You fall to the level of your systems."[20] Create habits and rituals to recharge, reset, and expand your capacity—physical, mental, spiritual, and emotional—for brave action.[21] If you think you've got too much on your plate to write in a journal or go for a run or do whatever helps you bring your bravest presence to your biggest challenges and *summum bonum,* you need to consider the possibility that you've got too much on your plate *not* to.

. . . .

I once heard it said that God had a dream and wrapped your body around it. Honor the "earth suit" that brought you into this world and enables you to make your imprint on it. Don't shortchange yourself of sleep. Move often. Consume more of what makes you stronger—from clean food to spiritual wisdom—and less of what doesn't. And although I'm no personal stylist, dress for the person you're on your way to becoming, not the person you were last year.

> Move the way love makes
> you move. Courage is love in
> its highest form.

"Don't move the way fear makes you move," wrote Rumi. "Move the way love makes you move."[22] Courage is love in its highest form. The paradox of courage is that you can be both tender and determined, daring and nervous, vulnerable and strong, *all at the same time.*

Embodying courage will never be a one-and-done. As you practice bringing your full presence to serve the highest good, your fear will lose its potency and your courage will grow. So do yourself a favor right now: pause from your doing and connect to the source of your being.

Breathe in courage.

Breathe out fear.

Breathe in courage again.

Now stand tall, fully present in your power, ready to step forward toward your highest good, radiating your light so brightly that it illuminates the light in others.

No Haka required.

STEP 4

Step into Discomfort

When I was growing up on a farm in the Aussie bush, our entertainment options were largely outdoors. For several years, my parents couldn't afford to fix our television (which only had three channels anyway), so it was very much a create-your-own-fun childhood. When I was about eight, I began ~~asking~~ pestering my dad for a pony. Yet as I already shared, years of drought had forced him to sell his dairy herd, which left little money for horses. So Dad sold a few pigs to buy an old horse instead. Roby arrived on the back of a rusty cattle truck on my tenth birthday. As I looked up at him, his 14 hands (56 inches at the shoulder) towering over ten-year-old me, I was utterly intimidated by his size. So much for a cute little pony. As daunted as I felt, I was equally determined to learn to ride him. So every morning before school, I'd head out to the paddock and attempt to saddle up. After school, I'd do it all again.

In the beginning, a subtle nausea would accompany me out to the back paddock. Yet day after day, week after week, my fear waned, and my confidence grew. By my eleventh birthday, I was wishing old Roby had more get-up-and-go. And so began my next campaign: for a faster horse. But the drought was wearing on . . . and on . . . money was tighter, and there were now six kids to feed and no pigs to spare. This time Dad entered a horse raffle: twenty cents a ticket or six for a dollar. One for each child! And I did the only thing I thought might improve my odds—I prayed. Or, more accurately, I bargained.

Dear God, if you help me win this horse, I promise I'll stop teasing my sister, avoiding helping Dad in the dairy, and stealing from Mum's secret stash of chocolate.

While I'm told that God isn't one for bargaining, on that fateful day he must have taken pity on me. Dad had the winning ticket! Or, more precisely, my little sister Anne's name was on the ticket, but she was only two. (Dear Anne, I owe you a horse.)

This time, it wasn't the size of my new horse—whom we named Smokey—that intimidated me. It was his sheer wildness. A frisky and freshly broken brumby from Australia's rugged Snowy Mountains, Smokey went from a standing still to a full gallop in five seconds flat, often leaving me on the ground behind him. But once again, I was determined: I would not let my fear of falling off keep me from saddling up. And sure enough, as the weeks rolled into months, my courage grew along with my skill in the saddle. Within eighteen months, I was competing, occasionally even winning, local barrel races.

My years of learning to ride held a valuable lesson for life: growth and comfort can't ride the same horse.

> Growth and comfort can't
> ride the same horse.

At first pass, a life of pure comfort holds appeal. Yet when all we do is what's comfortable, we deprive ourselves of what's possible, cutting ourselves off from the very experiences that would build our confidence and enrich our lives. In today's modern world where comfort is easily purchased, we run the risk of living a life of immaculate mediocrity, failing to honor the opportunity we have to live a more meaningful and rewarding one. Not only that, but each time we take the easier option, our comfort zone constricts, gradually shrinking our confidence to do anything that requires stepping out of it. The lesson: comfort doesn't stay comfortable forever.

You can't grow when you're putting nothing on the line. Growth requires exertion. Exertion isn't comfortable. When psychologist Abraham Maslow was developing his hierarchy of needs for human motivation, his most profound finding was that the level a person was on was less indicative of their happiness than the effort they were exerting to grow to meet higher level needs.[1] And so too for you. It's the process of having to dig deep, learn new skills, handle disappointment, navigate unknowns, cope with rejection, and learn from failure that infuses a deeper dimension to your living and expands your psychological muscles for life itself. Overused as the caterpillar-to-butterfly metaphor may be, it captures how the friction in our lives, which forces us to struggle and disrupts our status quo, is essential for our development, growth, and ultimate flourishing. As research psychologist Barbara Fredrickson detailed in *Positivity*, it is the ratio of positive to negative emotions that we need to be mindful about, not the avoidance of negative ones.[2]

But here's the rub: the moment you step up to the threshold of your courage gap, you just might have a panic attack. Short of that, you may experience a sharp wave of nausea as butterflies go bonkers in the pit of your belly. Or a Mack truck parks on your chest. Or maybe that's just me. In any case, when your inbuilt threat alarm can detect any whiff of danger, it signals throughout your body: retreat! What to do?

Remember, your body and emotions are inextricably linked. Your brain interprets excitement the same way it interprets anxiety. Psychologists at Stanford University found that shifting your mindset to embrace stress as important for learning, growth, and bringing your A-game to the challenge at hand changes the body's physiological response to stress and helps build your capacity for dealing with future challenges.[3] The researchers concluded that people with meaningful lives have more stress than those with less meaningful lives. So when you feel stress, interpret it as a signal that you're growing into your potential and as a barometer for how bravely you're living your life. Just because you feel nervous doesn't mean you're a wimp. It means you're on center court!

Emotions are the waves you navigate as you sail through life, but you are the captain. Or as Harvard psychologist Susan David says, "Emotions are data, not directives."[4] Your emotions are informing you how your internal state is reacting to an external stimulus, but it's up to you how you interpret and respond to that data. Whenever you face something unfamiliar, it can feel scary, but that doesn't mean you're not wholly capable of stepping forward. Most the time your discomfort is a prompt to press forward, not to escape. It's *because* you feel fear that you must practice courage. Courage is risking the comfort you have now for the future you want most.

> Your emotions are there to
> inform you, not to command you.
> Embrace discomfort as a cue to
> step forward, not to escape.

Before stepping on a stage to speak, my throat clams up and I sometimes feel a sudden urge to race to the bathroom. Rather than wish my nerves away (or visit the bathroom), I've learned to reset my relationship to my discomfort, embracing it as a sign that I'm exactly where I'm supposed to be, on center court in my life, growing into my potential and living out my purpose. The same is true for you. You cannot will away discomfort—your clammy hands, dry throat, or nauseous pangs of vulnerability. Rather, utilizing the power of language, you can transform your experience of the moment by shifting how you're interpreting it. As surfing champion Mark Matthews said, "I just fell in love with that feeling you get from being terrified."[5]

What you resist persists.[6] By giving yourself permission

to feel anything, it liberates you to do everything. By surrendering resistance and embracing the discomfort, you can refocus on what brought you to this moment:

The good you want to do. The change you want to make. The person you want to be.

> Trade the comfort you have now
> for the fulfillment you want most.

I once attended a boot camp where we routinely had to hold a plank for one minute. Starting out, I'd collapse to my knees after about eight seconds. But over time, as my core strengthened, I worked up to the full one minute (albeit the longest sixty seconds of my day). Learning to hold a plank for one minute taught me that I can do anything hard one minute at a time. I called this my "one-brave-minute" rule, and it has led to countless great experiences and opened many doors.

> Courage is a muscle. You
> have to put in the reps and
> "train the brave" within you.

After moving to the Washington, DC, area (the first time), I was invited to an event where I didn't know a soul—not even the person who invited me. I made a deal with myself to brave thirty minutes. If I hadn't met anyone by then, I'd go home.

As has usually been the case when practicing my one-brave-minute rule, I met a fabulous woman as I walked in the door, and by the time I left two hours later, I'd been invited to run a "courageous conversations" workshop at NASA headquarters. No kidding. I ended up running many leadership programs there. The lesson: your life will expand in proportion to how often you risk one brave/uncomfortable minute. And sure, not every brave minute will land a new relationship or opportunity, but any brave minute could. Yet even when it doesn't, it builds your courage muscles for the next one. Literally.

> Reframe risk to factor in the timidity tax of playing it too safe. Sticking with what's comfortable may be the very reason you don't have something better.

Making courage a habit takes repetition, not perfection. There is hard science behind the old saying "You are what you repeatedly do." *Long-term potentiation* (LTP) is a form of neuroplasticity in which every action you take—your input—builds neural connections in your brain based on receptor patterns of activity that create long-lasting change in output.[7] The adage "Neurons that fire together, wire together" explains how your brain's pathways grow from goat tracks to highways when you put in the reps—starting with the first rep. Put five hundred words on paper. Walk four thousand steps. Do three push-ups. Make five cold calls. Speak twice at every meeting. Risk seven rejections. Run three minutes. Lift five pounds. Or fifteen. Work up from there. To quote Charles Dickens, "The sun itself is weak when it first rises and gathers strength and courage as the day goes on."[8]

What's known as the "mere exposure effect"—a phenomenon where repeated exposure to something shapes our perception of it beyond our conscious awareness—intersects with this. By voluntarily exposing yourself to situations that have historically made you afraid, you become more comfortable with feeling uncomfortable emotions, and over time, you can even come to seek out similar situations. The more you do, the more you expand your capacity for being comfortable being uncomfortable. For instance, before my first-ever television interview nearly twenty years ago, my knees were literally knocking together from nervousness to the point that I thought people might think I had a muscular disorder. My reaction has since scaled back to a dozen unruly butterflies doing backflips in my belly. By breathing into their flip-flops, I can at least get them flipping in formation. The same is true for you. No emotion lasts forever. Every feeling will pass. So if you're going to be uncomfortable, go all in. Double down on discomfort to hone your A-game for bigger pursuits. Your challenges won't get easier, but you'll grow braver in dealing with them. As Ginni Rometty, former chair and CEO of IBM, observed on her career journey, "Growth and comfort cannot coexist."[9]

In a world where much lies outside our control, it's easy to get uptight about risk. There are many. Yet not all risks are created equal, and many risks are less threatening if we take steps to reduce our vulnerability. A formula from Stan McChrystal helps make this distinction: Risk = Threat × Vulnerability.[10]

If there's a threat but no vulnerability, then there's no risk. For instance, if you're afraid of sharks (threat), but you only swim in a lake, you're not vulnerable to losing your leg to one—in which case, zero risk. If you happen to live by the ocean, you can reduce your vulnerability by not swimming at dawn and dusk when sharks are more active. Building on this is my formula for courage:

Courage = Action/(Fear + Risk)

This formula illustrates that courage is not defined by the absence of fear or eradication of all risk, but rather by the willingness to take action in their presence. As such, stepping into your courage gap neither denies legitimate threats nor seeks to make you invulnerable to them. Rather, it's about taking considered risks; doing what you can to mitigate your vulnerability to an outcome you *do not* want while still taking action to pursue the higher outcome that you *do* want. Deflating your fear and increasing your willingness to act are not only essential to changing situations that you *don't* like, they're indispensable for making the changes and taking the chances to create the circumstances you *do* want. As Robert Biswas-Diener wrote in *The Courage Quotient*, "living courageously is synonymous for living well." This requires leveraging two core systems in our brain: the *behavioral inhibition system* that keeps us on alert and feeds our fear as well as the *behavioral activation system* that drives us toward positive outcomes and goals.[11]

To that end, if you want to live a good life, you need to

regularly be taking action amid your fears and the potential risk of failure. Something that Amy C. Edmondson, of Harvard Business School, calls intelligent failure. "An intelligent failure occurs as part of what you believe is a meaningful opportunity to advance toward a valued goal," she wrote in *Right Kind of Wrong*.[12] Even if your actions fail to land your ideal outcome, they'll still move you forward because you'll have learned something and earned respect in the process, from yourself and likely from others too.

> When you are willing to feel anything, you embolden yourself for everything.

That's what happened in the early days of my relationship with Andrew. We'd been dating about two months when six words came out of his mouth that stopped me in my tracks: "I've fallen in love with you." Knowing he didn't have a disingenuous bone in his body, I stood looking at him like a deer in the headlights, thinking *Oh shit.* I knew he must have been hoping for a declaration of equal measure. But like him, I've never been one to say something I don't mean. "I really like you," was the best I could fumble out, feeling guilty as his eyes shot downward, likely to conceal his disappointment. "No, like I really *really* like you," I repeated, hoping the emphasis on the additional *really* would compensate for the absence of the big L-word. "Like a *really really* lot." He lifted his head, let out a sigh, and then with his dimpled smile he said,

"Well, I guess I'll just have to content myself with being *really* likeable." Ah, the magic of humor to soften a hard moment. Although I couldn't reciprocate his sentiment, I admired his courage. A lot. Sometime later, well after I had reciprocated, I asked why he'd decided to be so vulnerable, risking expressing his love so early in our relationship rather than waiting until he stood a stronger chance of the big-L response. "It's what felt true to me," he said, "and I felt too strongly about you not to share my truth with you. And if you'd run a mile, at least I'd have known where I stood."

Andrew is a relatively private guy, but he was OK with my sharing this story to underscore a pivotal message of this book: that your life will expand in proportion to your willingness to embrace the entirety of human emotions. Again, when you are willing to feel anything, it emboldens you for everything. In the process, it deepens your day-to-day experience of being alive and expands your capacity for those days that can wreak the most havoc on your heart.

Such is what I felt when I was finally able to return to Australia after two years of being unable to fly due to the impact on international travel from the COVID pandemic. Dementia had taken a heavy toll on my mum since we had last hugged goodbye in early March 2020. I will never forget her first words to me the first time I saw her. "Margaret Mary, is it really you? I feel like I am looking at myself, only younger," she said, staring at me like I was an apparition. It was a precious, poignant and yet painful moment. As her words and ailing mind yanked on my heart strings, I knew I had to allow myself to feel *every* emotion, *all* the way through. As life has repeatedly taught me, attempting to cherry-pick the emotions we feel not only cuts us off from our full humanity but confines us to living in the middle octave of life where we risk arriving at life's end with a whole unlived life still inside of us.

Whether in our personal or professional lives, we humans aren't wired to embrace the low notes—those uncomfortable and painful emotions that trigger our deepest vulnerability. We're wired for the exact opposite: to protect ourselves from pain. But the avoidance of suffering is a form of suffering. Similarly, only when you give yourself permission to feel your most painful and uncomfortable emotions *all the way through* can you liberate yourself to do the very things that would make you feel most alive. To launch that startup or scale that business. To call it quits or pursue a new endeavor or adventure or (fill-in-the-blank!) despite the unknowns.

Never discount the hidden and delayed timidity tax you pay when you don't risk stepping forward. Over the course of our lives, we fail far more from timidity than we ever do from overdaring.

Our time as hunter-gatherers wired our brains to be "uncertainty averse"; that is, we instinctively equate unknowns as potential threats.[13] It's why people find it more stressful not to know whether their position will be cut in a long-rumored restructure than to be told definitively that it will. It's also why you may have once put off making a decision that would have invited more uncertainty into your life, even when your logical brain knew it was the right thing for you to do. Or maybe you just took a really long time to finally take the leap or make the change and later wished you'd acted far sooner. The gravitational pull of the status quo is strong and change, even change for the better, is always unsettling to some degree, small, or dauntingly large. So even when the status quo is far from ideal, it's familiarity spares us the uneasy feeling that uncertainty provokes. After all, no front-page headline ever read "[Insert Your Name] Did Nothing."

> You can't make the right step
> without risking a wrong one. In a
> world advancing rapidly, cautious
> inaction can be a high-risk strategy.

Yet as life marches steadily forward, deciding to do nothing because you're not certain exactly what to do and don't want to deal with so many unknowns is not risk free. Sure, you may see little downside to staying where you are *right now*, but when you don't risk the uncertainty of that first step, you also don't learn, you don't grow, and you get precisely zero useful information to help you in taking a second step. Not only that, but every day you choose comfort over courage is a day you are not moving forward. A lost day. No discovery. No seeds planted. No doors knocked on, much less opened. Indecision is not free. Delay often grows increasingly expensive.

Indecision is ultimately a delaying tactic for avoiding the chance of failure. So interrogate your well-polished excuses. Life's best opportunities rarely come perfectly wrapped with a pink bow on top, in the perfect moment, and with a free-return-shipping guarantee. More often, they're wrapped a little messy, covered with question marks and without a user manual. But waiting for all those questions to be answered is a recipe for regret. The antidote to uncertainty is being certain that whatever happens, you can handle it. Life rewards action. Doing defeats doubts.

> Behave your way into believing.
> Doubt dissolves through doing,
> not thinking.

I'd never have embarked on a year backpacking around the world—across the US, Europe, and Southeast Asia—on my own after graduation had I not had the courage to leave home three years earlier to attend college. I'd never have had the guts to then backpack in Africa or around the Middle East had I not first traveled to less foreign places. I'd never have found the courage to move to Papua New Guinea at twenty-six had I not had the courage to do so much intrepid travel in the years prior. And I wouldn't have had the guts to launch a new career in a new country at thirty-four, with four kids under six, had I not built my capacity to act despite my fears from all the experiences that had come before.

Every experience that calls on you to step into your courage gap builds your capacity for bigger challenges and bolder endeavors. So don't spin yourself a tale that unless you "burn the boats" nothing else matters. Not true! Every single step, however small, however seemingly insignificant to anyone else, is a vote for the person you're growing to become. Even when a brave step forward doesn't land your ideal outcome, your decisiveness to act emboldens you in ways that indecision and procrastination never can. There is no greater antidote to fear than action in its presence. It's why you must not wait for courage, but decide to behave your way into believing. In the same way that you become a better swimmer by swimming or a better cook by cooking, you build your courage by "couraging."

. . . .

Many people spend their lives waiting to feel brave only to arrive at the end of their life and regret having risked too little and lived too safely.[14] Research on the "theory of regret" finds that we are three times more likely to regret the actions we did *not* take over those that we did.[15] Over time our psychological immune system can more easily justify an excess of courage over an excess of cowardice, even when our courage didn't land the outcome we'd hoped. Because when we cower to fear and do nothing—when we *don't* make that bet on our dream, when we *don't* go on that adventure, when we *don't* ask that person out for coffee, or choose to stay in our dead-end job or toxic relationship—we remain unchanged, often growing increasingly disconnected from our own passion, power, and potential. As Harvard psychologist Daniel Gilbert wrote in *Stumbling on Happiness*, "We hedge our bets when we should blunder forward."[16]

The gravitational pull of the status quo will always be working to keep you in place. As Robert Kegan and Lisa Lahey explain in *Immunity to Change*, despite our commitment to change toward a new desired state, there is a strong underlying pull—a countercommitment—to preserving the status quo that's operating beyond our conscious awareness. As Kegan and Lahey suggest, an X-ray of our immunity to change would resemble the top secret playbook of a national defense system.[17] Such is our hypersensitivity to any perceived threat to our status quo. Think of it as an internal tug-of-war playing out between your highest desires and your deepest fears, between your ego's need to *look good* and win applause and your heart's need to *do good* for a cause greater than ourselves. If you're clear about what your deepest self *really* wants, then going out on a limb is the safest place to be.

As you take that first step into discomfort, take your patience with you. Just as the cost of being too cautious is rarely immediate or obvious, the same is true of the benefits of being brave. It took nearly a hundred years for the suffragettes to win the right for women to vote in the US. It took James Dyson fifteen years and 5,126 failed prototypes to invent the bagless vacuum cleaner. And it will take you more than one brave minute to do something amazing. So be patient—just because you can't see the fruits of your courage right away doesn't mean they're not coming!

Stepping into discomfort requires shifting from a defensive "play not to lose" fear mindset to a proactive "play to win" courage mindset. The fear mindset is focused on the downsides and protecting against loss and scarcity, fearcasting worst-case scenarios. It fosters indecision and smothers the creativity and the bold leaps necessary for breakthroughs, rendering you more vulnerable to the very outcomes that this mindset seeks to avoid.

By contrast, the courage mindset is fueled by a bold vision

and a big why. It's grounded in growth and purpose-driven commitment to a higher good. It's focused on possibilities over probabilities, it embraces experimentation, and reframes risk through a long-term lens that recognizes what is put at risk if you *don't* step into the courage gap. In doing so, it turns fear (of what you put at risk by being too cautious) into a catalyst for transformative growth. It's the mindset of every single successful person. As Ginni Rometty said in Korn Ferry's Women CEOs Speak, "One of the biggest decisions is to get comfortable with risk-taking. That is when growth happens."[18]

Embracing the discomfort and difficulty inherent in achieving a worthy goal helps people to stay the course, in contrast to those who think it should be easy. As a study of women on a weight-loss program found, the women who assumed they'd easily succeed lost an average of twenty-four pounds less than those who expected it to be tough.[19] I'm putting this principle to work as I train for my first marathon, embracing my tired legs in the knowledge that achieving this long-held aspiration won't be easy and will take many uncomfortable steps and hard miles. By the time you read this, I hope to have crossed the finish line. If I haven't, I'll be rereading Step 5!

Greta Gerwig, the director of *Barbie, Little Women,* and *Lady Bird* (my favorite), was rejected by every single graduate film school. She's now one the most sought-after film directors in the world. A little further back in history, George Washington was defeated on the battlefield more times than he won, and Abraham Lincoln lost eight elections before winning the presidency. Likewise, Theodor Seuss Geisel, known to generations as Dr. Seuss, had his first book rejected by twenty-seven publishers, and the first time Jerry Seinfeld stepped on stage, he froze and was jeered off. Yet he returned the next night.

People who reach the mountaintop didn't just fall there. What sets them apart is not superior intelligence. (I'm pretty sure Seinfeld would tell you that!) Millions who boast a high IQ live uninspired lives, captive to their fear of appearing less than brilliant. What distinguishes the most rewarding lives is a learner's curiosity coupled with a willingness to continually risk not nailing it; to experiment with different approaches yet remain undefined by their missteps. After all, you can't yield the results of an experiment without risking the experiment! If you don't allow room to get it wrong, you'll never get it right.

> Aim to maximize your learning,
> not to execute every step perfectly.

"Our success at Amazon is a function of how many experiments we do per year, per month, per week, per day," said Jeff Bezos, who says he often makes decisions based on 70 percent of the desired information and believes the smartest people are those who are smart enough to know they aren't smart enough to have all the right answers, so they're constantly learning.[20] Viewing every step as part of a grand experiment is powerful because, in experimentation, failure does not exist. Experiments are really the ultimate source of certainty because each guarantees a new learning. By relieving you of the pressure to get it right, experiments free you to take more action. And in a world that's changing so fast that it's hard to imagine what it will look like in ten years, much less fifty, embracing an experimental mindset accelerates your learning curve enabling you to adapt more quickly and do better.

Of course, embracing experimenting won't dissolve all fear. But that's not the goal. The goal is to move forward despite how you feel in any given moment, choosing courage over comfort, growing gradually more comfortable being uncomfortable. This little role play may help:

Fear says: I'm just not sure I've got what it takes. Others seem so much more talented.
Courage says: I have everything it takes to get started, and I'll get better as I go along.

Fear says: But what if I get it wrong and mess it up?
Courage says: Yes, that could happen, but without risking getting it wrong, I will never get it right!

Fear says: I'm not even sure where I'm headed. My plan is still in pencil.
Courage says: Perfect! I don't need to know the destination, just the direction. The only step that matters is the one immediately ahead. The rest will become clear over time.

Fear says: But it feels safer to stay put for now. There are just so many unknowns.

Courage says: I'm not waiting for certainty. A year from now I'll be glad I didn't delay. The best opportunities will emerge from stepping forward despite my unanswered questions.

And if fear yanks you down the "What if?" rabbit hole— *What if I'm not good enough? What if the market tanks? What if I lose my job, my business, my everything?*—dial up your courage to full volume and ask: *How likely is this to happen? What would I do if it started to happen? What's at stake if I let fear win?*

> Don't just risk growing pains, embrace them. The alternative: a slow slide to death.

Legend has it that in the battle for Texas's independence in 1836, Colonel Travis pulled out his saber and drew a line in the sand for his men defending the Alamo. He told them they'd likely die fighting General Santa Anna and his army, so they were free to leave. But if they wanted to stay, they needed to step over the line in front of them. Despite the odds, every man stepped over that line, caring more for their comrades and cause than for protecting their own lives.

Over history, millions have chosen to step forward and risk their lives for a noble cause. And many still do today. Chances are you don't need to risk your life, but as you stand on the edge of the rest of your life, you *will* need to decide what you value more than comfort:

Will you risk the discomfort of stepping toward what you most want—or not?

Just as cold water doesn't get warmer if you jump in later, putting off an uncomfortable step won't make it easier to take a year from now. The reasons driving your hesitation won't magically vanish, but the price you'll pay for giving them so much weight will go steadily up.

Abraham Maslow wrote, "You can choose to go back toward safety or forward toward growth. Growth must be chosen, again and again. Fear must be overcome again and again."[21] With each step you take—however small, imperfect, and uncomfortable—you are investing in the person you have it within you to become. Courage is walking with fear, not fear eradication. So as you think about the courage gap that divides where you are from where you want to be, let me ask you:

If not now, then when? If not you, then who?

Don't just mentally answer these questions, physically *act* on them. Make the most important bet you can ever make: on yourself. Take one small step in the direction of the future you want to create and the person you want to become—for yourself, for those you care about, and for the world in general. Will every step move you forward? Unlikely. If you knew every shot would hit a bull's-eye, it would not be worth the effort. More important than getting every step perfectly right is never having to look back and wonder, "But what if I'd tried?"

As Admiral Bill McRaven shared in his commencement address at the University of Texas, "we all have lines in the sand, boundaries we must protect, values we must uphold."[22]

Similarly, we all have fears that keep us from stepping bravely forward. Rarely do we defeat our fear in one fell swoop. Rather, we defeat fear in a succession of a thousand smaller, sometimes nerve-racking, but always life-affirming steps.

We human beings can do anything for one brave minute at a time. So here is another mini-experiment to try: be brave for just one minute before bed tonight. Just one measly minute. Notice what happens. Notice what does *not* happen. Notice how it sets you up for a better tomorrow.

. . . .

Now, a quick recap of Steps 1 through 4.

You've clarified what you most want and are focused on who you most want to be.

You've rescripted your story to recast yourself as the author and hero of your life, wholly equipped to go after what you want, change what you *don't want*, and do brave things.

You've inhaled courage—from yourself, from others—and are standing tall in the power of your presence (looking a million bucks, I might add!).

And now you're embracing discomfort as a cue to step forward into your courage gap, inspired for the possibilities ahead.

Perfect timing for a Taylor Swift quote, "I think fearless is having lots of fears but jumping anyway."[23]

Jumping into your courage gap won't be comfortable. You might want to throw up. You might trip and sprain your ankle. But it's the scary work that wins the day and tips the scales in your favor. No plank required.

STEP 5

Find the Treasure
When You Trip

efore I walked onstage to give the opening keynote at an educational leaders' conference, the head of the association, a prominent leader in education, stepped up to the podium to open the event. I was expecting the usual courteous remarks. A welcome, a few words on the importance of education. The usual stuff. I was wrong.

As she began to speak, it was clear she had something more pressing to say. "I want to share a mistake that I made this year," she announced. At once, the room was at full attention. She went on to explain how she'd exercised poor judgment on a sensitive issue several months earlier, how she'd been presumptuous and had failed to ground her assumptions with a sufficiently broad group of stakeholders. She had responded swiftly to their feedback, but it had been a jarring experience. "What I've learned is that I need to spend more time asking questions and listening for how I might be wrong. But while I failed in that instance, I am committed to not failing to learn the lessons my failure held, confronting as they were." She went on to say how the experience had strengthened her resolve to lead with the humble curiosity and courage that she wanted to inspire in students. As she finished speaking, several people stood to applaud. Then a few more, and more, until everyone was on their feet. It was a powerful moment that set the stage for my address on leading with courage. Her vulnerability—to own her failure and share its lessons—exemplified courageous leadership.

The truth is that all of us will trip up on our journey through life. To be human is to fail. Regularly. At least if you're living a full life. I say this not to discourage but to liberate. Because once you accept that you are certain to fail, you can choose *how* you fail, enabling you to fail smarter and rise stronger. After all, there's a vast difference between twenty years of experience and living the same year twenty times, tripping over the same things with each lap around the sun.

Your failures will fall into one of two buckets:

- *Bucket 1:* You will try and fail to get your desired result.
- *Bucket 2:* You will fail to try.

Both varieties hold valuable lessons. Herein lies the problem, however—as hard as it is to fail, it's even harder to learn from our failure.[1]

> To be human is to fail. Your job
> is to make each failure worthy
> of the person you're on your
> way to becoming.

Sometimes we put this down to complex causes—which is valid in some instances. But the biggest impediment to learning from failure is not its complexity but we ourselves. We resist confronting failure honestly because failure disrupts the story we like to tell about ourselves. So we airbrush over it, we dismiss it, we deflect it, and we rescript the story we're spinning to protect our ego and make ourselves feel better about it. All of which prevents us from finding the treasure when we trip, mining its nuggets of precious learning.

Step 5 in closing your courage gap requires resetting your relationship with failure to become its student rather than its victim. Only then can you counter the psychological immune reaction you have to failure and mine the lessons every failure—of outcome or effort—in order to learn, to grow, and, to quote Henry Ford, "to move forward more intelligently."[2] The alternative? Business as usual. Continuing as before, spinning vital lies to feel better about yourself and missing out on the condiment that gives success its flavor. As Kathy

Calvin, former president and CEO of the United Nations Foundation, told me: "We all make mistakes; it's what you do next that matters most." Which brings us to a fundamental principle for success in every realm of life: failure is an event, not a person.

> It is how you explain your failure
> that determines future success,
> not the failure itself. Failure is an
> event, not a person.

Who you are is not your failures. Not your past failures. Not your future failures. Not a current failure you're disentangling your way out of right now. As positive psychology experts Martin Seligman and Peter Schulman from the University of Pennsylvania found in their research, it is how we explain our failures—our "explanatory style"—that's the key determinant of our future success, not the nature or size of the failure itself.[3] History is awash with examples.

Although Henry Ford is remembered for pioneering automobile production, his legacy was forged through failure, most notably the bankruptcy of his Detroit Automobile Company. But Ford never gave failure the power to define him. Rather, by analyzing his missteps, he laid the foundation for the Ford Motor Company. Ford's explanatory style is reflected in his belief that "the only real mistake is the one from which we learn nothing."[4] A century later, fellow pioneer on the ground and into space, Elon Musk, echoed a similar philosophy: "If things aren't failing, you're not innovating enough."[5] Study anyone who has accomplished something remarkable and you'll find a common pattern: they never view failure as defeat but as an opportunity to do better. On the flip side, you are also not defined by your success. Not your past success. Not your future success. Not by your reputation or job title or latest win or any other external mark of merit. Although it's tempting to build your identity on what you do or achieve, particularly when you're really good at it, if your identity rests in what you accomplish, you risk living your entire life feeling insecure. Rather, you are intrinsically worthy by no other virtue than by simply being born. Period. This is true despite your failures, your flaws, and any other work-in-progress parts of you that you'd prefer kept hidden. We all have them.

> Befriending failure won't fracture your self-esteem; it will fortify it.

This is a big truth. The biggest. If you've internalized experiences in ways that have hung a question mark on your innate worth, it may take some time for this truth to seep in. The likelihood that an earlier version of yourself will be arguing otherwise doesn't alter the big-T Truth that even if you never do one significant thing with the rest of your life (which is highly unlikely given you're motivated enough to read this book), you are still worthy. Period. The beauty of knowing that you're not defined by anything you do—or fail to do—liberates you to take more steps into the gap between where you are and where you want to be, in service of your *summum bonum.*

So let's begin with how to rise stronger and wiser from Bucket 1 failures—from the times you've been brave, but your best efforts have fallen short or landed you flat on your derrière.

It's a well-worn maxim that failure is a stepping stone to success. True, but there's a catch. Sure, you need to regularly risk failure if you want to succeed at something new. As former IBM CEO Thomas J. Watson said, "If you want to increase your success rate, double your failure rate"[6] Yet risking failure, even the intelligent kind, is only half the golden ticket to success and making something of your life. The other half of the ticket is your willingness to learn, to apply, and to generously share the lessons your failures hold.

No one sets out to fail. So when you put yourself "out there"—risking your money, reputation, security, time, and social or political capital—and it does *not* pay off, it can be discouraging, if not outright jarring, to how you like to see yourself and be seen by others. Yet this is where your work in Step 1 bears rich fruit. Because when you are clear on what you most want, failure won't send you into a shame spiral or to spinning "vital lies" to protect the image you have of yourself. Nope. When you are clear about what you most want— to *do* and to *be*—your failures will compel you to reflect honestly what you did, or failed to do, even unintentionally. Only by taking responsibility can you respond constructively.

"The ego is the sworn enemy of learning and growth," wrote Ryan Holiday in *Ego Is the Enemy.*[7] In its need to look good or to avoid looking bad, our ego erects a barrier to learning. The more we become ensnared in our image of success, the more sensitive we grow to anything that might tarnish it, making the barrier to learning even more formidable. Professor Sydney Finkelstein at Dartmouth University found that senior leaders are *less* likely than those further down an organizational hierarchy to consider themselves as a source of failure and *more* likely to defend, dismiss, and deflect responsibility for unwanted outcomes.[8] We cannot learn from failure when we're preoccupied with touching up or protecting our self-esteem.

> Never let a failure go to waste.
> You can't control the output of
> your efforts, but mining failure's
> lessons improves future input.

Too often we focus too much of our attention on what is outside our control and put too little focus on what lies within it. Given that you can only ever control the input, not the output, toward any goal, mining the output for nuggets of learning helps you upgrade future input. The further you progress on your chosen path, the more vigorously you must analyze your failures. This isn't to blame yourself but to better yourself and model the way for others. That's exactly what Microsoft CEO Satya Nadella did in the aftermath of a remark he made at a women's engineering conference. Asked for his advice to women who weren't comfortable asking for a raise or promotion, he answered that they should "trust karma," suggesting that the system would ultimately reward their work. The backlash was swift. Yet rather than be defensive, Nadella immediately owned his mistake and apologized. "I was completely wrong," he said, publicly sharing the valuable lesson he'd learned and role-modeling the growth mindset he'd committed to embedding across Microsoft.[9] Taking ownership for his misstep was walking his talk, "We need to be a company of 'learn-it-alls' not 'know-it-alls." As Carol Dweck, whose book *Mindset* inspired Nadella, has said, "Everyone is a work in progress."[10]

In the aftermath of the infamous flop of Virgin Cola, Richard Branson prioritized time and resources into examining what they got wrong, ultimately concluding that they'd strayed from their core mission, which was to significantly improve on what the market was already offering. He didn't let that failure go to waste but mined every ounce of learning it held. Branson's relationship with failure is a key contributor to his success as it is for every successful entrepreneur. "The best lessons are usually learned from failure. You mustn't beat yourself up if you fail—just pick yourself up, learn as much as you can from the experience, and get on with the next challenge."[11] Which brings me to Bucket 2 failures: failing to try.

When my first book, *Find Your Courage*, was published, I sent a box of them to Oprah at her Chicago production studio, where she was still doing her daily talk show. I had low expectations of hearing anything back, so it wasn't surprising when I didn't. Every author on the planet wanted to be on Oprah's show, and I was as no-name as they came.

Then one day, a few months later, something remarkable happened.

I was leaving a meeting at a hotel in Washington, DC, a copy of *Find Your Courage* in my bag, and as I walked past the front reception desk, none other than Oprah's best friend, Gayle King, walked into the lobby to check in.

> Learn to forgive the part
> of you that wimps out.

Suddenly time stood still. My brain sprang into overdrive. *This is my moment*, I thought. My chance to give Gayle a copy of my book to pass along to her bestie. I was mere steps from my portal to every author's version of a golden ticket.

Yet there I stood, frozen, watching Gayle—who appeared weary and focused on getting to her room. *Do I? Don't I?* Intellectually I knew I had absolutely nothing to lose. Worst case, Gayle would throw my book in the trash. So it was a no-brainer to take the four and a half steps across the atrium to politely ask if she'd pass my book along to Oprah. But in that *Do I? Don't I?* moment—my fear and courage in a full-fisted bar brawl—my fear of being intrusive and feeling awkward won out over my desire to give my book a fighting chance of helping millions.

And so there I remained, motionless, as Gayle took her room key and walked to the elevator.

Ticket-shmicket. Courage-shmourage. Oprah Shmoprah.

My inner critic went ballistic. *You are pathetic. You totally wimped out. You don't deserve to be on Oprah!* For a long time afterward, I turned that fleeting moment of cowardice into a baton for beating up on myself. I told no one (until you, now). I felt ashamed. After all, how could I claim to help people be braver if I'd yet to master my own inner wimp?

The part of me that's scared to feel the sting of rejection lives on and strong. However, as I've grown better at listening to the voice in my head feeding wimp pellets to my inner Chicken Little—I've gotten better at taking a deep breath and embodying my inner Braveheart. Think Elsa from *Frozen*. *Most of the time.* Every so often my inner wimp still wins out.

If we humans didn't wrestle with fear and sometimes lose, there'd be no need for courage. Our moments of standing on the edge of our courage gap, computing pros and cons, debating *Do I? Don't I?* often occur in a fraction of a second. And when we shame ourselves when our fears win out, we not only shut down our inner Braveheart but we avoid risking future failure. It's why closing your courage gap requires your making peace with your inner wimp, befriending the fear that's trying to protect you from pain.

"I'm always courageous," said no one ever. Your fear—in all its many guises . . . pride, procrastination, doubt, "judgyness," shyness, insecurity, your urge to control and polish the details to perfection—will sometimes get the upper hand.

To be human is to coexist with a gap between who you are being and who you can be, between what you're doing and what you can do. This isn't something to beat yourself up about. Layering a negative judgment onto a fact or feeling improves nothing. Counterintuitive as it may feel, your bravest action and highest contribution flow from accepting your fallibility, not resisting it. It is through embracing your vulnerability—to the lowest instincts of your nature and the outer forces of life—that you access your source of greatest strength and summon deeper reserves of courage to rise over fear.

Of all the antidotes to failure—whether failure to land our desired result or our failure to be brave in critical moments—none holds more potency than practicing self-compassion; forgiving ourselves for being the fallible human beings that we are. Research by self-compassion expert Kristin Neff found that in extending more compassion to ourselves—particularly in our fallen moments when negative emotions run amok—we are less afraid to take risks and access our innate resilience. After all, if you don't have the tools to get back up, you won't risk falling down. As Kristin shared on my podcast, "Our voices of self-criticism aren't trying to hurt us but are a misguided effort to protect us. Yet we can't grow better by beating ourselves up."[12] Likewise, research into posttraumatic growth found that by embracing our humanity with compassion, we can find purpose in our suffering and grow into a more connected, positive, grateful, and wholehearted human.[13]

Try. Rise. Fall. Learn. Grow. Try. Fall again . . . the path toward all human progress was also the path of Alex Pease.

For several years, Alex sought to rationalize his behavior to preserve his esteem and avoid failing again. A leadership program he attended was the catalyst for him to confront his ego's self-protective instinct and forgive his fallibility. "Realizing that vulnerability is a strength, not a weakness, was a slow journey," he said. As he dismantled the shell that he had erected to protect himself, he came to know—at a level transcending the intellect—how his ultimate source of security could never come from avoiding vulnerability, but rather by embracing it.

> Forgive the younger version of
> yourself who could not have
> known what you've since learned.

"It took me a long time to look forward and not look backward; to use the experience to live the highest purpose for my life and become a force for good versus a force for punishing myself." Had other factors been at play on that fateful day? Absolutely. No behavior exists in a vacuum. Yet it was by taking full responsibility for what he chose *not* to do— regardless of the pressure he felt—that he was able to shed his shame and move forward as the wholehearted man and servant leader he wanted to become.

"Learning to let go control has been terrifying yet liberating," admitted Alex, whose passion for fostering an empowering culture for the fifty-five thousand employees in his company to achieve their potential speaks more loudly than any words. He is also passionately committed to supporting fellow veterans in finding new purpose and embracing their full humanity as they transition to civilian life. "I made a commitment when Jason died never to let that happen again. It took me a while to learn that while I could not control everything, I could choose never to let my lack of courage be the reason for not doing what I can to make things better for others."

To be clear: self-forgiveness is not a "get out of jail free card" for wimping out when you know you need to step forward. Rather, it's about sparing you the futility of shaming yourself in both the moments you try and fail and the moments you fail to try. You can't elevate yourself while berating yourself. That's why, in a culture that pressures us with perfectionist ideals while touting self-acceptance, one of the bravest acts is to accept yourself—for who you are, for who you're not, and for often falling short of being the person you most aspire to become. Shaming yourself never leads to bettering yourself. Only love can do that.

Make peace with your
unfinished self.

For much of my adult life, whenever I was feeling down on myself, I could count on my mum for encouragement. "Oh darling, don't be so tough on yourself," she'd say. "You're doing a wonderful job managing all you do. We all slip up. Be a little gentler to yourself." When the thick, brutal fog of dementia rolled in over her mind and body, I was forced to develop more self-reliance in being kinder to myself in hard moments. At Mum's funeral, people spilled out the back of the church in the rural community where I'd spent my childhood. I knew that Mum had never been particularly social, but I'd underestimated the impact she'd had on so many people. As we celebrated my mum's life, there was one word above all others that people used in describing her.

Grace.

Mum exuded that hard-to-define yet you-know-it-when-you-feel-it quality of grace. Her gentle way of being was never overpowering, but always left people feeling heard and seen, particularly those who felt the least heard and seen. Although I've often marveled at the contrast of our personalities—me an extrovert and Mum the polar opposite—I've always tried to emulate a little of the grace she exuded with such ease. "Grace, like water, always flows to the lowest part," wrote Philip Yancey.[14] In doing so, it ultimately lifts us higher. As you extend grace inward, give an extra-generous serving to the critical part of yourself that is quick to point out your shortcomings.

After Mum's funeral, my three sisters and I went through a stack of old boxes gathering dust on the top shelf of her wardrobe. They were filled with the keepsakes—old cards and letters, newspaper clippings, wedding invitations—we save for "one day" that never comes. I popped a few into the back sleeve of my journal, where I promptly forgot them. Then, not long ago, a clipping from her church bulletin slipped out from my journal and floated serendipitously onto my lap. On it was a prayer titled "Patient Trust" by the French Jesuit priest Pierre Teilhard de Chardin. The last line struck a deep chord: "accept the anxiety of feeling yourself in suspense and incomplete."

I have a feeling that de Chardin's encouragement to "accept the anxiety of feeling yourself in suspense and incomplete" may be for you as well as me. We are each incomplete, innately fallible, and as vulnerable to the lower instincts of our nature as we are to the outer forces of the world. The sooner we can accept that there will always be a tension between who we are being and who our deepest self is calling us to be, the less tense and more content we become. So before trying to fix whatever problems you're facing, try forgiving the earlier version of yourself that could not know what you've since learned. Doing so will not only help you find the treasure when you trip, accruing wisdom to trip less often, but also liberate you to step into your courage gap more consistently.

No irony was lost on me that while I was writing this book, an opportunity to step into my own gap presented itself, time-traveling me right back into that DC hotel lobby. Except this time, instead of Oprah's best friend, it was America's First Lady. Let me back up a little.

I'd recently had my request to US Citizenship and Immigration Services (USCIS) to expedite renewal of my "travel parole" rejected, preventing me from traveling to India as a senior advisor to the CEO Institute[15] without canceling my application for a green card. It also meant I would have to wait out the USCIS's fourteen-month processing time before I could leave the country to visit my dad and family in Australia. Feeling deflated and frustrated, I decided to do what has always helped me in difficult situations, particularly when my own efforts felt futile: I prayed.

Early the next morning, I walked to my local exercise studio and lo and behold, as I stepped into the class right in front of me was the wife of the US president, First Lady Dr. Jill Biden. After exchanging a warm hello, I proceeded to work out beside her. All the while my brain was racing. *Is this God's way of helping me out of my travel pickle? What are the odds?!* I felt that speaking to her directly would be disrespectful and rude. When she walked out of the studio a little early, my internal fear/courage wrestling match went into overdrive. *Should I walk out and ask her security people to give her a message? Everyone in the class will think I'm weird. I'll look like a stalker.* My Oprah-Gayle frozen moment fresh in my mind from writing this book, I made the decision: *I will not let fear win!* Embracing my "one-brave-minute" maxim, I exited the class to ask one of her security detail whether he could pass on a message. "I'm sorry, ma'am," he said, very Secret Service–like. "I'm not able to do that, ma'am. Best to go through the official channel. Have a nice day, ma'am." I thanked him politely and walked back into the class, feeling extremely self-conscious and awkward yet proud of myself for winning that wrestling match.

> The world has never sought your infallibility. It seeks only your courage.

When I got home, I sent an email through the White House website, identifying myself as "the woman beside you who needed to work on her plank," explaining my predicament and asking, ever so politely, if she might be able to help. I figured the odds were low, but if God was trying to answer my prayer, I needed to do my part. Well, lo and behold again, a week later an official email from the White House landed in my inbox stating that they'd passed along my request to the USCIS. The following week, it was approved. Although the paperwork didn't arrive in time for my trip to India (freeing up time to write this book!), it returned my travel freedom and reaffirmed a core message of this book: your life will expand in proportion to your willingness to feel awkward. Equally important, making peace with your unfinished self and befriending your fear won't make you wimpier, it will make you braver. (I should add that prayer can help too! Thank you, JC.)

Novelist F. Scott Fitzgerald observed that "the test of a first-rate intelligence is the ability to hold two opposed ideas in the mind at the same time, and still retain the ability to function."[16] This is never truer than when it comes to stepping into your courage gap:

- You have all the courage you need to pursue what you most want.
- You will often fail to be as courageous as you'd like.

Your courage gap will never be fully closed, or not for long. And it's not supposed to. Because the point is not about arriving on the other side. The point is to embrace the journey itself—in all its mystery and messiness, complete with the full spectrum of human emotions that weave contrasting threads to create the masterpiece that is your life. As Father Richard Rohr recently shared with me at Modern Elders Academy, true maturity is to live peacefully with life's contradictions in an imperfect world. I think it is also the ability to forgive our imperfect selves and make gentle peace with our deepest fears.

"The cave you fear to enter holds the treasure you seek," wrote Joseph Campbell on how best to pursue your individual hero's journey.[17] So as you finish the fifth step, my wish for you is never to feel "finished" but to continue your inward exploration as you pursue higher ground, peeling back the veils of fear that keep your light from shining your brightest.

This world needs your courage, not your perfection. So whatever emotions you are feeling—inspired or apprehensive, committed or uncertain—I invite you to take one small step forward into your courage gap. And then tomorrow, repeat. However small or imperfect each step may be, I have not one iota of doubt that you will always be glad you took it. There are many all around you who need it. Now more than ever.

When you trip up, as you inevitably will (maybe by dinner), forgive yourself for being the rough draft of the person you're on your way to becoming. Only then can you bring the full quota of your flawsomeness (no, this is not a typo; it's linguistic experimentation) to what and whom you care about most, making the one-of-a-kind imprint that only you can make.

Make Others Braver

G o on, just do it!" my friends yelled through cupped hands from the ground below.

"Find your courage. Stop playing safe. You've got this!"

I got their joke, but I couldn't manage a smile. There I was, high above them on a trapeze platform, utterly frozen at the prospect of reaching out to grab the trapeze bar. Intellectually I knew I should just lean in and go for it. After all, I was strapped into a harness with a safety net below. But in that moment, I felt paralyzed by fear of falling to my death.

No irony was lost on my friends that I'd written books for such moments. It's why I could hear the smiles in their voices as they shouted my book titles up at me.

Perhaps it was fear of professional humiliation prevailing over fear of falling to my death, but their encouragement was just the nudge I needed to reach out, grab the bar, and, letting out one almighty scream, swing out for my Cirque du Soleil moment. The seconds that followed confirmed what I'd long suspected: I was never meant to run away and join the circus.

We all have moments when we know what we should do but are hesitant to do it. And it's in those moments that a few words of encouragement can make all the difference. It's why closing your courage gap begins in your mind, but it doesn't end there.

Just as each cell in our body is like a battery, we are each a cell in the larger body of humanity. When one cell lights up, it illuminates those around it. As they light up, they radiate light further still. It's why with each passing lap around the sun since my days singing "Luceat Lux Vestra" in my high school choir at Nagle College, I've grown more inspired by its motto. Latin for "Let Your Light Shine," it came from Jesus's teaching to "Let your light shine before others" (Matthew 5:16, NIV). The imagery of shining our light brightly and into the dim places around us speaks directly to the desire within each of us to aspire toward our highest good.

"I just feel too encouraged," said absolutely no one I've ever met. But I do regularly meet people who are starved for encouragement, including people you might assume have long outgrown any need for it. Encouragement is like verbal sunshine. We need it to blossom. This is why you can likely recount a time when someone's encouragement was just what you needed to move forward. Maybe a teacher or one of your earlier managers recognized potential in you that you'd yet to appreciate in yourself, buoying your confidence to defy your doubts. Or perhaps someone reframed the risks, helping you fully appreciate what you were putting at stake if you played it safe, emboldening you to take the leap you'd been putting off.

Or perhaps you felt like giving up on your road less traveled, and a few well-timed words of encouragement helped you go that extra mile when the hard yards counted most.

> Fear may be contagious,
> but so too is courage.

If not for my friends bellowing up at me that day under the high top, I'd have climbed back down. Same again the time my family decided to climb Mt. Kilimanjaro. On summit day there were many occasions I felt like throwing in the towel and descending back to base camp. The thin air had my head throbbing, my heart pounding out of my chest, and my stomach so nauseated I vomited the one granola bar I'd managed to eat. But we had all committed to climbing to the "rooftop of Africa" to mark Andrew's fiftieth birthday, so I pressed on. We *all* pressed on. One glacially slow step after another, lifting one another up, encouraging one another forward, until nine grueling hours after we set off, we reached the summit. That climb held many lessons on grit, teamwork, and leadership. But perhaps the most poignant can be encapsulated by the African proverb: If you want to go fast, go alone. If you want to go far, go together.

This is true for every worthwhile endeavor. Although many feel pressure to sharpen their elbows and view success as a zero-sum game in which another's gain is their loss, the truth is that we rise higher and advance further when we lift others along our path. The ancient wisdom of Saint Thomas

Aquinas, who observed that *Bonum est diffusivum sui*—"the good is self-diffusive"—has been validated by modern science. Research into the "open loop" of our limbic system has proven how emotions spread irresistibly whenever people are in proximity to one another.[1] In our workplaces, we literally "catch" emotions from one another—from anxiety to ambition, anger to optimism.[2] One study found that when three strangers sat facing one another in silence for just one minute, the most emotionally expressive person transmitted their mood to the other two—without a single word being spoken.[3] It's through the invisible threads that tie us to one another that we can disentangle our insecure, fearful selves, summoning our courage and dialing up our light.

> It's through the invisible threads that tie us to one another that we can disentangle our insecure fearful selves.

Every revolution and remarkable achievement throughout history has shown how courage begets courage, spreading contagiously from one person to another. Anytime a group is bound by common purpose and emboldened to risk failure to achieve it, what they can accomplish far exceeds the sum of their parts. On the flip side, every decline and disaster can be traced back to decisions guided by fear. The largest threat to any group or enterprise is never external but rather the fear that resides in its midst, nodding compliantly in meetings, hiding silently behind screens, buttoning up behind scripted rhetoric, or "polishing the apple" upward to avoid the fallout from communicating a less shiny truth.

Those privileged to hold leadership roles have an amplified impact on—and responsibility for—the collective mood and emotions lower on the ladder, acting as thermostats to set the emotional climate. Yet a lack of positional power is no excuse not to use your personal power to influence change from whatever rung you're on. As Daniel Goleman, Richard Boyatzis, and Annie McKee point out in *Primal Leadership*, "Not all 'official' leaders in a group are necessarily the emotional leaders."[4] In our celebrity-obsessed culture that is quick to put people up on pedestals and treat them as idols, be careful not to make others too big and yourself too small, overvaluing who you're not and undervaluing who you are.

> Measure yourself by how
> brave you make others feel.

Whether you aspire to lead at scale or simply want to lead yourself better, you have the power to help others be braver. And it's important that you use it. Not just for the sake of the people close around you, but for the state of your own heart.

. . . .

1939–2023

That was the span of the life of my beautiful mother, Maureen Patricia (Brannigan) Kleinitz. And although it's nice to think that you might be the exception, one day a dash will mark the span of your own. Clearly, you didn't get much say in the circumstances of your arrival. But you are 100 percent responsible for the choices that will shape the person you will have ultimately become upon your departure. Nothing—no accomplishment or fame or wealth—will impact the shape of your life and heart more profoundly than what you do to help others toward their own *summum bonum.*

> Your ability to lift people up and effect positive change begins where your comfort zone ends.

Just imagine if every person you knew—particularly those you'd like to admire—measured their success by how brave and empowered they made others feel. We'd be living in a safer world, working in stronger organizations led by better leaders, enjoying more authentic and constructive conversations, and emboldening a braver generation to steward the world thirty years from now. Although we humans are wired more for self-preservation than for self-actualization, every single day you can help others to close the gap between what they're doing and what they can do, between who they are being and who they can become.

You may be thinking, *Hang on a minute—I've yet to close my own gap, so let me do that first.* If you are, consider how the people who've inspired you most have not been invulnerable to fear but rather have committed themselves to their unique path of progress over perfection. Likewise, it's not your perfection people crave; it's your commitment to bringing your bravest self to all that you do and to those you do it with.

There are countless ways you can help the people you live and work with to step into their courage gap (quite apart from shouting book titles!). All of them will ultimately fall into one of the two domains for building courage mentioned in the introduction and elsewhere in this book:

- You can help to lower their fear—reframing their perceptions of danger, challenging the story that's fueling their anxiety and helping them feel safer to express vulnerability.
- You can help them increase their willingness to act—supporting their dreams, affirming their talents, encouraging them to take the leap and assuring them you've got their back.

> Encouragement is like verbal sunshine. We all need a regular dose to blossom.

Of the many ways you can help others feel braver, these three form a strong foundation for all others—affirming potential, creating safety, and modeling how to fail well and rise strong.

Affirm potential and possibilities

As a parent who has been launching four children into Adult-land over recent years, I know that the instinct to protect those we love from the risks and ravages of life runs strong. However we must not let it overshadow our desire to support those around us from forging their own unique path, despite the potential potholes we worry they'll fall into. Just as you've learned from your missteps, so too they have their own lessons to learn.

Our fear of what could go awry can easily undermine how supported we make people feel. If all you do is focus on what might go wrong, you enlarge the holes in others' psychological safety net, fueling their fear and siphoning their courage. So speak in ways that expand, not shrink, what people see as possible for themselves; help them walk taller and feel calmer, not more stressed. And if you worry that they've not adequately considered the risks, ask them how they plan to manage them. Your role isn't to dissuade people from stepping into their own courage gap; it's to help them navigate it wisely.

Maya Angelou is often quoted as saying, "People won't always remember what you said or what you did, but they will always remember how you made them feel."[5] Someone in your orbit would love to know that you believe in their ability to do hard things, achieve a bold goal, and handle the pressures that come with pursuing it. Cheer loudly. Share an inspiring article or podcast. Pass on this book. Give them a public shout-out. Drop them a text to affirm their gifts and dispel their doubts. Tell your waiter they've been amazing. Compliment a complete stranger on their smile or style!

Make vulnerability safer

Whenever organizations ask me to do a keynote speech or facilitate a program on scaling the courage mindset, I routinely do a briefing with the CEO, group leader, or event planner. Although the contexts differ, there's a remarkable consistency in what they ask me to help with: We want people to adopt a growth mindset, to think bigger and be bolder—to challenge old thinking, embrace change, and lead at every level. We want them to leave excited about taking our company to the next level. We want them to live our values . . . courage, collaboration, innovation . . . more honest candor, less blind compliance.

All worthy objectives. Yet most people default to playing it safe unless they feel totally safe to do otherwise.[6] Fear always stands in the gap between the espoused and lived values in any group. A lack of shared purpose widens it further. When the fear mindset is scaled, it creates environments in which everyone feels less secure and more vulnerable. Think Boeing. NASA *Challenger*. *Deepwater Horizon*. Volkswagen. Each of these disasters can be traced back to decisions governed more by fear of what could go wrong than by commitment to make things more right. As a CEO recently shared with me, every business failure he's ever encountered can be traced to one single factor: fear.

Fun fact: *Fear* is the most used word in the Bible racking up a whole 365 mentions. I'm no theologian, but my interpretation of this remarkable factoid is that our highest and holiest work requires overcoming our fear every single day of the year. (With a day off every leap year!)

123

The cognitive calculus will always err toward *me/now*—to say nothing, hide mistakes, and avoid upsetting the apple cart—rather than *we/later*, unless a stronger force is at play. It's why psychological safety—defined as an environment of shared vulnerability in which people feel safe to take interpersonal risks—is the strongest predictor of high-performing teams, more significant than collective IQ, education, or any diversity metric.[7] As Amy C. Edmondson, who coined the term *psychological safety*, shared with me, "Courage and psychological safety are two sides of the same coin."[8] Each time you reward brave behavior over outcome or respond well to bad news and critical feedback, you counter people's natural hesitation to take a risk or express an unpopular opinion.

> Share the setbacks and struggles your ego would prefer kept hidden. You inspire courage by modeling it.

Role-model how to fail well

You wouldn't have faulted Alex Pease had he chosen to keep his personal journey to himself, because you would never have known about it. Yet Alex's commitment to his *summum bonum*—"to be a force multiplier for good"—was greater than any inclination to shield himself from judgment. He shared his journey of learning to embrace vulnerability as his ultimate source of security in the hope that it would help others—maybe you—on their own inner voyage. As brave as Alex was during his time as a SEAL, it is the courage he has shown far from dangerous places that his greatest heroism has shone through. And so it is for all of us: it is through embracing our vulnerability that we become most opened to life and being a force multiplier for good in the lives of others.

If you only share your wins and the highlight reel of your career or life, you deprive others of benefiting from the hard-won treasure you picked up along your way. It's through sharing your setbacks, struggles, and the still-in-progress parts of yourself that you connect most deeply and inspire most authentically. As you do, you help others shed any shame they've attached to their failures, liberating them to reset their sights, rescript their story, and step into their lives more powerfully.

> Change happens in circles
> not rows. Each time you make
> someone braver, you make
> humankind better.

Human nature may be unchangeable, but we humans would not be here today if not for our unique capacity to change how we think and act and to better our lives. And while we often look to other people to be the hero to improve our lot in life, the hero we most need to step up to the courage plate in bigger ways is the person staring back at us in the mirror. There is, within the DNA of every one of us, our own heroic courage to create an extraordinary life and leave a unique legacy. That courage called explorers to venture west, over mountains, into deserts, across seas, over icecaps. It called uneducated workers to elevate the oppressed and educate the ignorant. And it calls you to boldly step up to the plate in your life to make others' hearts bigger and humankind better.

Change happens in circles, not rows. As you finish this book, I hope you'll take one brave action that will cast a vote toward the highest good for your life and, by default, everyone else's. And then tomorrow, another.

With every brave forward step, you will not only expand your own horizon of possibilities but amplify the ripple effect that inspires others to larger and more meaningful possibilities of their own. To quote Rainer Maria Rilke: "I live my life in widening circles / that reach out across the world. / I may not ever complete the last one, / but I give myself to it."[9]

Focus on your deepest desires and the highest good.

Rescript what's kept you scared and living a smaller life than is serving you or others.

Breathe in courage, standing tall in your full presence and in the power of our connectedness.

Step into discomfort—again and again and again.

Find the treasure when you trip, and make peace with your unfinished self.

Finally, *encourage others* to live and lead more bravely, ever widening the circles of courage rippling out across the world.

Notes

PREFACE

1. This quote is attributed to Mahatma Gandhi.

INTRODUCTION

1. Deborah L. Finfgeld, "Courage as a Process of Pushing beyond the Struggle," *Qualitative Health Research* 9, no. 6 (November 1999): 803–14, https://doi.org/10.1177/104973299129122298.
2. "More People Are Taking Drugs for Anxiety and Insomnia, and Doctors Are Worried," *Wall Street Journal*, May 29, 2020, https://www.wsj.com/articles/more-people-are-taking-drugs-for-anxiety-and-insomnia-and-doctors-are-worried-11590411600.
3. Kristina M. Hengen and Georg W. Alpers, "What's the Risk? Fearful Individuals Generally Overestimate Negative Outcomes and They Dread Outcomes of Specific Events," *Frontiers in Psychology* 10, no. 1676 (2019), https://doi.org/10.3389/fpsyg.2019.01676.
4. Hannah E. Jones, Julie A. Chesley, and Terri Egan, "Helping Leaders Grow Up: Vertical Leadership Development in Practice," *Journal of Values-Based Leadership* 13, no. 1 (2020): Article 8, https://doi.org/10.22543/0733.131.1275.
5. Viktor E. Frankl, *Man's Search for Meaning* (Boston: Beacon Press, 2006).

STEP 1

1. Claire E. Robertson, Nicolas Pröllochs, Kaoru Schwarzenegger, Philip Pärnamets, Jay J. Van Bavel, and Stefan Feuerriegel, "Negativity Drives Online News Consumption," *Nature Human Behaviour* 7

NOTES

(March 16, 2023): 812–22, https://doi.org/10.1038/s41562-023-01538-4.

2. "How Stress Affects Your Vision," Stress.org, American Institute of Stress, June 27, 2022, https://www.stress.org/news/how-stress-affects-your-vision.

3. Greg Miller, "Why We Walk in Circles," *Science*, August 9, 2009, www.science.org/content/article/why-we-walk-circles.

4. I wrote extensively about my brother Peter's journey with mental illness in *You've Got This!* (Hoboken, NJ: Wiley, 2020).

5. D. H. Lawrence, *Studies in Classic American Literature* (New York: Penguin Classics, 2021).

6. C. G. Jung, *The Collected Works of C. G. Jung: Revised and Expanded Complete Digital Edition,* ed. Gerhard Adler et al. (New York: Routledge, 2023).

7. Mitesh S. Patel, David A. Asch, and Kevin G. Volpp, "Framing Financial Incentives to Increase Physical Activity among Overweight and Obese Adults," *Annals of Internal Medicine* 165, no. 8 (October 18, 2016): 600, https://doi.org/10.7326/L16-0280.

8. Daniel Kahneman, *Thinking, Fast and Slow* (New York: Farrar, Straus and Giroux, 2011), p. 305

9. John A. Sturgeon and Alex J. Zautra, "Social Pain and Physical Pain: Shared Paths to Resilience," *Pain Management* 6, no. 1 (2016): 63–74, https://doi.org/10.2217/pmt.15.56.

10. Michael Kardas, Amit Kumar, and Nicholas Epley, "Overly Shallow? Miscalibrated Expectations Create a Barrier to Deeper Conversation," *Journal of Personality and Social Psychology* 122, no. 3 (2022): 367–398, https://doi.org/10.1037/pspa0000281.

11. James G. March, *A Primer on Decision Making: How Decisions Happen* (New York: Simon & Schuster, 1994).

12. This quote is attributed to Abraham Lincoln.

13. Zakary L. Tormala and Derek D. Rucker," Attitude Certainty: Antecedents, Consequences, and New Directions," *Advances in Consumer Research* 44 (2017): 176–80, https://doi.org/10.1002/arcp.1004.

14. Richard E. Boyatzis, "Unleashing the Power of Self-Directed Learning," in *Changing the Way We Manage Change,* ed. Ronald R. Sims (New York: Quorum Books, 2002), p. 25.

15. This quote is attributed to Lily Tomlin.

STEP 2

1. This quote is attributed to Ernest Hemingway.
2. Nassim Nicholas Taleb, *The Black Swan: The Impact of the Highly Improbable* (New York: Random House, 2007).
3. The concept of "vital lies" is attributed to Henrik Ibsen.
4. Daniel Kahneman, *Thinking, Fast and Slow* (New York: Farrar, Straus and Giroux, 2011), p. 220.
5. Emily Pronin, David Y. Lin, and Lee Ross, "The Bias Blind Spot: Perceptions of Bias in Self versus Others," *Personality and Social Psychology Bulletin* 28, no. 3 (2002): 369–81, https://doi.org/10.1177/01 46167202286008.
6. Deanna Kuhn, "How Do People Know?" *Psychological Science* 12, no. 1 (2001): 1–8, https://doi.org/10.1111/1467-9280.00302.
7. This quote is attributed to Daniel Kahneman.
8. Jim Loehr, *The Power of Story: Change Your Story, Change Your Destiny in Business and in Life* (New York: Free Press, 2008), p. 5.
9. Gardiner Morse, "Hidden Minds," *Harvard Business Review*, June 2002, https://hbr.org/2002/06/hidden-minds.
10. Statistics comparing risk of gun death in the US (excluding suicide) versus death by Australian deadly creatures were based on 2019 data from the CDC that shows approximately twelve deaths by gun per one hundred thousand per annum in the US annually relative to approximately six to seven deaths per annum nationally (twenty-five million people) from the top five deadly creatures in Australia (sharks, crocodiles, snakes, spiders, box jellyfish) (https://www.cdc.gov/nchs/pressroom/sosmap/firearm_mortality/firearm.htm).
11. Kristina M. Hengen and Georg W. Alpers, "What's the Risk? Fearful Individuals Generally Overestimate Negative Outcomes and They Dread Outcomes of Specific Events," *Frontiers in Psychology* 10, no. 1676 (2019), https://doi.org/10.3389/fpsyg.2019.01676.
12. This quote is attributed to Desmond Tutu.
13. Agnieszka Bober, Ewa Gajewska, Anna Czaprowska, Agnieszka H. Świątek, and Monika Szcześniak, "Impact of Shyness on Self-Esteem: The Mediating Effect of Self-Presentation," *International Journal of Environmental Research and Public Health* 19, no. 1 (2021): 230, https://doi.org/10.3390/ijerph19010230.
14. This quote is attributed to Henry David Thoreau.

STEP 3

1. The All Blacks have a 76 percent winning record in their 120-year history. "Who Are the All Blacks," https://www.experienceall blacks.com/insider-information/who-are-the-all-blacks.

2. Jeff Thompson, "Embodied Cognition: What It Is & Why It's Important," *Psychology Today*, February 20, 2012, https://www.psych ologytoday.com/us/blog/beyond-words/201202/embodied-cogni tion-what-it-is-why-its-important.

3. Bruce Lipton, *The Biology of Belief: 10th Anniversary Edition* (Carlsbad, CA: Hay House Inc., 2020).

4. Gavin de Becker, *The Gift of Fear: And Other Survival Signals That Protect Us from Violence*. (New York: Dell Publishing, 1998).

5. Cynthia L. S. Pury, "Can Courage Be Learned?" in *Positive Psychology: Exploring the Best in People*, ed. Shane J. Lopez, vol. 1, *Discovering Human Strengths*, 109–30 (Westport, CT: Praeger, 2008).

6. John, Amodeo, "Our Issues Live in Our Tissues," *Psychology Today*, December 2021, https://www.psychologytoday.com/us/blog/intimacy -path-toward-spirituality/202112/our-issues-live-in-our-tissues.

7. Bessel van der Kolk, *The Body Keeps the Score: Brain, Mind, and Body in the Healing of Trauma* (New York: Penguin Books, 2015), p. 105.

8. Anna Lugg, Mason Schindle, Allison Sivak, Hatice Tankisi, and Kelvin E. Jones, "Nerve Excitability Measured with the TROND Protocol in Amyotrophic Lateral Sclerosis: A Systematic Review and Meta-Analysis," *Journal of Neurophysiology* 130, no. 6 (December 1, 2023): 1480–91, https://doi.org/10.1152/jn.00174.2023.

9. Andrea Zaccaro, Andrea Piarulli, Marco Laurino, Erika Garbella, Danilo Menicucci, Bruno Neri, and Angelo Gemignani, "How Breath-Control Can Change Your Life: A Systematic Review on Psycho-Physiological Correlates of Slow Breathing," *Frontiers in Human Neuroscience* 7, no. 12 (September 6, 2018): 353, https://doi.org/10.3389/fnhum.2018.00353.

10. This quote is attributed to Ronald D. Siegel.

11. This quote is attributed to John Wooden.

12. Pablo Briñol, Richard E. Petty, and Blair Wagner, "Body Posture Effects on Self-Evaluation: A Self-Validation Approach," *European Journal of Social Psychology* 39, no. 6 (August 19, 2009): 1053–64, https://doi.org/10.1002/ejsp.607.

13. S. Nair, M. Sagar, J. Sollers III, N. Consedine, and E. Broadbent, "Do Slumped and Upright Postures Affect Stress Responses? A

Randomized Trial," *Health Psychology* 34, no. 6 (2015): 632–41, https://doi.org/10.1037/hea0000146.

14. L. Huang, Adam D. Galinsky, Deborah H. Gruenfeld, and Lucia E. Guillory, "Powerful Postures versus Powerful Roles: Which Is the Proximate Correlate of Thought and Behavior?" *Psychological Science* 22, no. 1 (2011): 95–102, https://doi.org/10.1177/0956797610391912.

15. Sreenath Nair, Meghana Sagar, John Sollers III, Nicholas Consedine, and Elizabeth Broadbent, "Do Slumped and Upright Postures Affect Stress Responses? A Randomized Trial," *Health Psychology* 34, no. 6 (2015): 632–41, https://doi.org/10.1037/hea0000146.

16. Shelley E. Taylor, Lien B. Pham, Irwin D. Rivkin, and David A. Armor, "Harnessing the Imagination: Mental Simulation, Self-Regulation, and Coping," *American Psychologist* 53, no. 4 (1998): 429–39, https://doi.org/10.1037//0003-066x.53.4.429.

17. James E. Driskell, Cindy Copper, and Aidan Moran, "Does Mental Practice Enhance Performance?" *Journal of Applied Psychology* 79, no. 4 (1994): 481–92, https://psycnet.apa.org/doi/10.1037/0021-90 10.79.4.481.

18. Marshall Goldsmith, *Triggers: Creating Behavior That Lasts— Becoming the Person You Want to Be* (New York: Crown Business, 2015), p. 21.

19. André P. Lauer, "What I Learned about Presence and Power from the Haka," *Medium*, June 6, 2020, https://medium.com/@andre.p .lauer/what-i-learned-about-presence-and-power-from-the-haka-d2 351c7aa3f0.

20. James Clear, *Atomic Habits: An Easy & Proven Way to Build Good Habits & Break Bad Ones* (New York: Avery, 2018), p. 27.

21. Chapter 5 of my book *You've Got This!* (Wiley, 2020) is dedicated to rituals and habits that build capacity for taking action.

22. This quote is attributed to Rumi.

STEP 4

1. Abraham H. Maslow, "A Theory of Human Motivation," *Psychological Review* 50, no. 4 (1943): 370–96.

2. Barbara Fredrickson,. *Positivity: Top-Notch Research Reveals the Up-ward Spiral That Will Change Your Life* (New York: Crown Publishers, 2009).

3. Alia J. Crum, Peter Salovey, and Shawn Achor, "Rethinking Stress: The Role of Mindsets in Determining the Stress Response," *Journal of*

Personality and Social Psychology 104, no. 4 (2013): 716–33, http://dx.doi.org/10.1037/a0031201.

4. Susan David, "The Gift and Power of Emotional Courage," TED video, November 2017.

5. Red Bull, "Mark Mathews: Red Bull Wingfinder Results," December 2018, https://www.redbull.com/us-en/mark-mathews-red-bull-wingfinder-results.

6. This quote is attributed to Carl Jung.

7. Michel Baudry, "Long-Term Potentiation (Hippocampus)," in *International Encyclopedia of the Social & Behavioral Sciences*, 2nd ed., ed. Neil J. Smelser and Paul B. Baltes (Elmsford, NY: Pergamon Press, 2001), 14: 9081–83.

8. This quote is attributed to Charles Dickens.

9. "IBM's Ginni Rometty: Growth and Comfort Do Not Coexist," *Fortune*, October 5, 2011, https://fortune.com/2011/10/05/ibms-ginni-rometty-growth-and-comfort-do-not-coexist/.

10. Stanley McChrystal, *Risk: A User's Guide* (New York: Portfolio Penguin, 2021), p. 10.

11. Robert Biswas-Diener, *The Courage Quotient* (Hoboken, NJ: John Wiley & Sons, 2012), p. 3.

12. Amy C. Edmondson, *The Right Kind of Wrong: The Science of Turning Failure into Success* (New York: Atria Books, 2023), p. 53.

13. Dan Grupe and Jack Nitschke, "Uncertainty and Anticipation in Anxiety: An Integrated Neurobiological and Psychological Perspective," *National Review of Neuroscience* 14 (2013): 488–501, https://doi.org/10.1038/nrn3524.

14. Bronnie Ware, author of *Five Regrets of the Dying*, on my *Live Brave* podcast, episode 75, August 17, 2020.

15. Rik Pieters and Marcel Zeelenberg, "A Theory of Regret Regulation 1.1," *Journal of Consumer Psychology* 17 (January 22, 2007): 29–35, https://doi.org/10.1207/s15327663jcp1701_6.

16. Daniel Gilbert, *Stumbling on Happiness* (New York: Vintage Books, 2006).

17. Robert Kegan and Lisa Laskow Lahey, *Immunity to Change: How to Overcome It and Unlock the Potential in Yourself and Your Organization* (Boston: Harvard Business Review Press, 2009).

18. "Journeys to the Top: How Women Reached the CEO Role," Korn Ferry, accessed June 26, 2024, https://www.kornferry.com/insights/featured-topics/diversity-equity-inclusion/journeys-to-the-top-how-women-reached-the-ceo-role.

NOTES

19. Gabriele Oettingen and Thomas A. Wadden, "Expectation, Fantasy, and Weight Loss: Is the Impact of Positive Thinking Always Positive?" *Cognitive Therapy and Research* 15 (April 1991): 167–75, https://doi.org/10.1007/BF01173206.

20. Jeff Bezos and Walter Isaacson (Contributor), *Invent and Wander: The Collected Writings of Jeff Bezos* (New York: Harvard Business Review Press, 2020), p. 73.

21. Abraham H. Maslow, *Motivation and Personality*, 2nd ed. (New York: Harper & Row, 1970), p. 98.

22. William H. McRaven, University of Texas Commencement Address, May 17, 2014.

23. This quote is attributed to Taylor Swift.

STEP 5

1. Laura Kreis-Winkler and Ayelet Fishbach, "You Think Failure Is Hard? So Is Learning from It," *Perspectives on Psychological Science* 17, no. 6 (May 17, 2022): 1511–24, https://doi.org/10.1177/17456916211059817.

2. This quote is attributed to Henry Ford.

3. Martin Seligman and Peter Schulman, "Explanatory Style as a Predictor of Productivity and Quitting among Life Insurance Sales Agents," *Journal of Personality and Social Psychology* 50, no. 4 (1986): 832–38, https://doi.org/10.1037/0022-3514.50.4.832.

4. This quote is attributed to Henry Ford.

5. This quote is attributed to Elon Musk.

6. This quote is attributed to Thomas J. Watson.

7. Ryan Holiday, *Ego Is the Enemy* (New York: Portfolio/Penguin, 2016), p. 104.

8. Sydney Finkelstein, "When Bad Things Happen to Good Companies: Strategy Failure and Flawed Executives," *Journal of Business Strategy* 26, no. 2 (April 1, 2005): 19–28.

9. "Microsoft CEO Satya Nadella's Gaffe on Women and Raises," *Vox*, October 9, 2014.

10. Andrew Hill, "Psychologist Carol Dweck: 'Everyone Is a Work in Progress,'" *Financial Times*, December 6, 2019, https://www.ft.com/content/fd3e920e-0f7d-11ea-a7e6-62bf4f9e548a.

11. "Turn Failure into Success: Sir Richard Branson + Tyra Banks," YouTube video, posted by Google for Startups, June 18, 2019.

12. Kristin Neff on my *Live Brave* podcast, episode 12, October 10, 2018.

13. Lesley Collier, "Growth after Trauma," *Monitor on Psychology* 47, no. 10 (November 1, 2016).

14. Philip Yancey, *What's So Amazing About Grace?* (Grand Rapids, MI: Zondervan, 2018), p. 6.

15. The CEO Institute is a program run by the CEO and Enterprise Leadership Development Practice at Korn Ferry International.

16. This quote is attributed to F. Scott Fitzgerald.

17. This quote is attributed to Joseph Campbell.

CLOSING

1. Howard Friedman and Ronald Riggio, "Effect of Individual Differences in Nonverbal Expressiveness on Transmission of Emotion," *Journal of Nonverbal Behavior* 6 (December 1981): 96–104, https://doi.org/10.1007/BF00987285.

2. Caroline A. Bartel and Rossana Saavedra, "The Collective Construction of Work Group Moods," *Administrative Science Quarterly* 45, no. 2 (2000): 197–231, https://doi.org/10.2307/2667070.

3. Howard S. Friedman and Ronald E. Riggio, "Effect of Individual Differences in Nonverbal Expressiveness on Transmission of Emotion," *Journal of Nonverbal Behavior* 6, no. 2 (1981): 96–104, doi:10.1007/BF00987285.

4. Daniel Goleman, Richard Boyatzis, and Annie McKee, *Primal Leadership: Learning to Lead with Emotional Intelligence* (Boston: Harvard Business Review Press, 2002), p. 9.

5. This quote is attributed to Maya Angelou.

6. Zorana Ivcevis, Jochen I. Menges, and Anna Miller, "How Common Is Unethical Behavior in US Organizations?" *Harvard Business Review*, March 20, 2020, https://hbr.org/2020/03/how-common-is-unethical-behavior-in-u-s-organizations.

7. Amy C. Edmondson, *The Fearless Organization: Creating Psychological Safety in the Workplace for Learning, Innovation, and Growth* (Hoboken, NJ: Wiley, 2018).

8. Amy C. Edmondson on my *Live Brave* podcast, episode 116, December 8, 2023.

9. Rainer Maria Wilke, from *Das Studenbuch* [*Book of Hours*], translated by Joanna Macy, (1899–1903, published 1905), https://writing.upenn.edu/library/Rilke_Book-of-hours.pdf.

Courage Gap Resources

Visit TheCourageGap.com or scan this
QR code to do the following:

- Take the Courage Quiz and assess your Courage Gap.
- Download The Courage Gap Workbook and apply the five steps to your life.
- Get Margie's free *Live Bravely* newsletter, latest videos, and episodes of the *Live Brave* podcast.

Courage Reflection Questions

Step 1: Focus on What You Want, Not on What You Fear

1. What does your deepest self want right now and in your life overall?
2. What is the bravest and most inspiring vision for your life?
3. Who do you most want to be as a person? List the values that will guide how you show up for life.

Step 2: Rescript What's Kept You Scared or *Too* Safe

1. What old story have you been telling that has not made you feel braver (failing the 3P test)?
2. What do you risk missing out on if you stick to that old story? Is the payoff worth the price?
3. What new story must you tell to pursue the highest good in your current situation—one that makes your courage greater than your fear?

Step 3: Breathe in Courage

1. If you were embodying courage today, how would you stand, walk, and talk?
2. What relationships and habits will you invest in to grow into your bravest self?
3. Where do you need firmer "courage rails" to shield yourself from people who don't make you feel braver (and maybe do just the opposite)?

Step 4: Step into Discomfort

1. Where can you apply the "one-brave-minute" rule today?
2. What do you risk regretting or missing out on if you don't take brave action?
3. What experiment do you need to try, giving yourself permission to not get it perfectly right?

Step 5: Find the Treasure When You Trip

1. What are your top three most valuable lessons from your greatest failures and where can you apply them today?
2. What past failure is still awaiting either forgiveness or ownership or both? Write a letter forgiving your younger self for what you had yet to learn.
3. How will embracing vulnerability and making peace with your "unfinished self" empower you to express yourself more authentically?

Bonus Questions: Help Others Be Braver

1. Who would value your encouragement today? Reach out to at least one person. Notice how encouraging them also encourages you.
2. How will you be more proactive and consistent in helping others feel braver and less anxious?
3. How can you model courage today by embracing vulnerability as a source of strength, not weakness?

Acknowledgments

I have many people to thank—not just for helping bring this book into the world but for helping me become the person who could write it.˙

My first and loudest shout-out must go to Andrew, my husband of thirty-one years and counting. It is a deep blessing to be "doing life" with someone who continually forgives the parts of me that are still "under refinement" and champions me to share my gifts and shine my brightest. While many have helped me be braver, your name sits top of the list.

Gratitude also to Jeevan Sivasubramaniam, my editor at Berrett-Koehler, for his wise guidance and encouragement throughout the writing process. To the whole purpose-driven team at BK and to Susan Geraghty at 1,000-Books—thank you for your expertise and professionalism in helping this book come together.

To Ange, what a gift it's been to have you as my VP of Everything for so many years across multiple continental moves. To Keri, what a blessing to have your support as I reset and relaunch! Also to Becky Robinson at Weaving Influence and Mark Fortier and the Fortier PR team—thank you for helping me broaden my reach and amplify the impact of this book in creating a better, braver world. To Marilee Haynes—thank you for your sharp eye and insightful feedback on this manuscript. Likewise, to Helen Ayres and James Tuttle for your input and encouragement!

To Lachlan, Kaitlyn (my daughter-in-love), precious Jireh, Maddy, Ben, and Matthew—it is my life's richest blessing to have you in it.

Thank you also to everyone who has championed me not just in writing this book, but in resetting my sails for the chapter ahead. To Anna, Mez, Chelle, Joan, Jamen, Cath, Anne, Preet, Susan, Suzi, Jo, Janet, Mary, and Jeanne—thank you for challenging my doubts and cheering me on as I've stepped into my courage gap. To my beautiful dad, Ray Kleinitz—my heart softens simply writing your name. In the midst of grieving the loss of the love of your life, you've never failed to lift me up, affirm my gifts, or say a prayer with me and *for* me. I know you've never been much of a reader and will unlikely read this book, but I know you're proud of me for writing it.

A special note of deep gratitude to Stan McChrystal for writing the foreword and to Alex Pease for trusting me to share his story. I cannot overstate how honored I feel and how much I admire your big and brave heart.

To every other big-hearted friend, relative, client, and colleague who has been a source of encouragement, thank you for extending me grace that I have not mentioned you by name. Please know how much I treasure your friendship and the light you bring into my life and into so many others.

My final acknowledgment is to God, in whom my ultimate security rests and from whom my deepest courage flows. It's my hope that this book honors the light God's given me to share in the world.

Index

Page numbers followed by fig refer to a figure on that page.

About the Author

MARGIE WARRELL, PhD, is a globally recognized authority in personal development and courageous leadership.

Since growing up as the big sister of seven on a farm in rural Australia, Margie has gained deep insight in the human condition and the fears that limit individuals (and organizations) from growing into their fullest potential and making their highest point of impact.

A sought-after keynote speaker who has spoken to thousands of audiences in over thirty countries, Margie is also a trusted C-suite advisor and consultant. Amazon, British Telecom, Deloitte, Google, L'Oreal, Marriott, Mars, Morgan Stanley, NASA, and Novartis are a few of the organizations who have sought her expertise to embolden braver leadership and build cultures of courage.

Margie's commitment to "braver leadership for a better world" extends to advising congressional chiefs in the US Congress and political leaders in developing nations, especially emerging female leaders. Her extensive experience across cultures, including that gained from her role as Senior Partner in Board & CEO Succession at Korn Ferry, informs her advisory efforts.

Host of the popular *Live Brave* podcast and a *Forbes* contributor, Margie regularly shares her expertise with leading media—such as CNN, Fox News, the *New York Times*, the *Today Show*, and the *Wall Street Journal*—and has lectured at numerous universities globally from Georgetown and USC to her alma mater Monash University in Australia. A LinkedIn Top Voice and member of *Harvard Business Review* Advisory Council, Margie also serves on the board of several not-for-profit organizations, including Women's Democracy Network and Forbes School of Business & Technology, dedicated to improving education, women's leadership, and female empowerment.

Outside work, Margie's love for adventure travel and hiking inspired her to climb Mt. Kilimanjaro with her husband and their four teenage children.

Margie lives in Old Town Alexandria, Virginia. Learn more about how she can support you, your organization, or your next event at at MargieWarrell.com. Connect on social media @margiewarrell.